Time and Mind in Wordsworth's Poetry

JEFFREY BAKER
St. Francis Xavier University, Nova Scotia

Time and Mind in

Wayne State University Press   Detroit 1980

Wordsworth's Poetry

Library of Congress Cataloging in Publication Data

Baker, Jeffrey, 1925–
   Time and mind in Wordsworth's poetry.

   Bibliography: p.
   Includes index.
   1. Wordsworth, William, 1770–1850—Criticism and
interpretation.   2. Time in literature.   1. Title.
PR5892.T5B3   821'.7   80-11947
ISBN 0-8143-1655-7

For Joyce

Contents

Acknowledgments

All quotations from *Wordsworth's Poetical Works*, edited by Ernest de Selincourt and Helen Darbishire (5 vols., 1940–49) and from *The Prelude*, edited by Ernest de Selincourt and Helen Darbishire (1959), are made by permission of Oxford University Press. I am grateful to Fr. R. J. MacSween of the English Department of St. Francis Xavier University for permission to reprint the first half of chapter 4, which first appeared as "Time and Judgement in 'The Ruined Cottage,'" *Antigonish Review* 1 (Autumn 1970):3–23. The second half of chapter 5 first appeared as " 'Deliberate Holiday': Wordsworth's Doctrine of the Necessity of Idleness," *Criticism* 13 (Summer 1971):242–64.

My thanks are also due to Christopher Hanson, F. N. Lees, and the late J. D. Jump, all of Manchester University, for criticism, advice, and encouragement in the early stages of this project. For very necessary practical help, I must thank the governors of St. Francis Xavier University, Nova Scotia, and J. T. Sears, dean of arts, for providing me with the comfortable leisure in which to bring this work to completion. A special word of thanks is also due to Christine Howlett for the speed and excellence of her typing and for her patience and skill in elucidating all the emendations of my original script.

Note on the Text

All Wordsworth quotations are from the de Selincourt-Darbishire editions of *Wordsworth's Poetical Works* and *The Prelude*. In the few instances where I have thought it necessary to help the reader locate a poem, *Wordsworth's Poetical Works* is cited as *P.W.*, followed by the volume and page number. Unless otherwise stated, all quotations from *The Prelude* are from the 1850 version.

1

Introduction

On the evening of their wedding day, William and Mary (Hutchinson) Wordsworth, while travelling westward across the Hambleton Hills in Yorkshire, were delighted by a particularly splendid cloud formation lit by the waning sun. Their eyes found pictures in the clouds—an Indian citadel, a Greek temple, a Christian abbey with bell tower, seas, islands, and groves. And yet, the poet says in the sonnet in which he records the experience, "we felt the while / We should forget them; they are of the sky, / And from our earthly memory fade away" ("Dark and more dark the shades of evening fell," *P.W.*, 3:25). The comment is deceptive; the reader supposes that a commonplace sentiment has been plainly expressed. But when we try to paraphrase the lines we find that there is a difficulty in them, and that it cannot be resolved. The ambiguities are not reconcilable; the meanings are not merely opposed but conflicting, and they are philosophical in nature. It is in fact the main statement of the poem we cannot get at, not a comment or an embellish-

ment. The trouble lies in the phrases "of the sky" and
"earthly memory." In this context "earthly" seems to mean
mortal, bodily, and is thus set against things "of the sky"—
that is, things of heaven, which are therefore thought of as
permanent. And yet we know that it is the cloud-capped
towers and solemn palaces that will fade, the insubstantial
pageant will dissolve in rain or be blown asunder by winds,
while the Wordsworths and the Hambleton Hills will endure
somewhat longer. We are therefore not sure what is the symbol of permanence and what the symbol of transience. Some-
time during the following eighteen months Wordsworth
wrote another sonnet, commenting on these last two lines
and using them as a necessary epigraph.

> —'they are of the sky,
> And from our earthly memory fade away.'
>
> Those words were uttered as in pensive mood
> We turned, departing from that solemn sight:
> A contrast and reproach to gross delight,
> And life's unspiritual pleasures daily wooed!
> But now upon this thought I cannot brood;
> It is unstable as a dream of night;
> Nor will I praise a cloud, however bright,
> Disparaging Man's gifts and proper food.
> Grove, isle, and every shape of sky-built dome,
> Though clad in colours beautiful and pure,
> Find in the heart of man no natural home:
> The immortal Mind craves objects that endure:
> These cleave to it; from these it cannot roam,
> Nor they from it: their fellowship is secure.
>
> (*P.W.*, 3:26)

According to lines 1–4 of this poem, the first interpretation
of the previous sonnet was the right one: the poet felt that the
clouds represented the permanence of spiritual life, while
"earthly memory" pertained to "life's unspiritual pleasures
daily wooed!" But, almost as if Wordsworth himself is seeing

the difficulty of the earlier sonnet for the first time, this reading is now overturned. Clouds, however splendid, are not the proper food of the human soul—"The immortal Mind craves objects that endure." And yet we are not really much further forward. For what are "objects that endure"? The Hambleton Hills, for example? These endure longer than the clouds, certainly, and longer than the Wordsworths too. Yet hills, clouds, and people are all in reality "earthly," and subject to change. Precisely what the "immortal Mind" craves depends on what we mean by "objects," and what we mean by "endure." Generally speaking we mean material things by "objects." If what the mind craves is material things that last a long time, then earth can supply them. But the very use of "endure" in connection with the cravings of "the immortal Mind" implies more than this. It suggests immutability, permanence, freedom from time. Wordsworth, in a sonnet intended either to clarify or modify the first poem, has in fact aggravated the difficulty.

This difficulty is not a matter of careless expression, nor even of attempting to define the ineffable. It is, rather, the product of sensations and hungers that are at odds with each other: the sense that the earth is solid and lasting is undermined by the coexisting sense that the earth is both gross and ephemeral compared to the permanence of heaven; a hunger for the visual splendors of earth and its pleasures is present with a hunger for the life of the spirit. It is a difficulty in fact proceeding from unfinished processes and inconclusive endeavors within the mind, struggles to find a satisfying and reassuring idea of what kind of a creature man is and what kind of a creation he dwells in. The need reveals itself in the dogmatic certainty of the phrase "immortal Mind," while the misgiving shows more subtly in the implicit contradictions in both poems, finally concentrated in the phrase "objects that endure." Wordsworth can hardly mean by it the abstract notion "objects of thought," since he is using it in antithesis to sense objects that do not endure—cloud formations and sunsets. But what in the world of objects does endure? Material objects are things of time; endurance is a property of "things of the sky."

The nature of this difficulty suggests that Wordsworth's mind was preoccupied by a scrutiny of the world of objects in what David Perkins has called a "quest for permanence."[1] His sensibility is permeated by his feeling of time, its processes and its forewarnings. This appears more clearly if we compare his account of the Hambleton Hills spectacle with that of his sister Dorothy, an observer less anxious about these matters.

> Far far off us, in the western sky, we saw shapes of Castles, Ruins among groves, a great spreading wood, rocks, and single trees, a minster with its tower unusually distinct, minarets in another quarter, and a round Grecian Temple also; the colours of the sky of a bright grey, and the forms of a sober grey, with a dome. As we descended ... we saw the wild and (as the people say) bottomless Tarn in the hollow at the side of the hill. It seemed to be made visible to us only by its own light, for all the hill about us was dark. Before we reached Thirsk we saw a light before us, which we thought at first was the moon, then Lime-kilns; but when we drove into the market place it proved a large Bonfire, with Lads dancing around it, which is a sight I dearly love.[2]

Dorothy seems almost as delighted by the tarn in the hollow of the hill, the bonfire and the young men dancing round it, as she is by the pictures in the clouds. She makes no distinction between things "earthly" and things "of the sky"; she pauses for no philosophical reflection, but hastens on, equally joyous and excited, to the pleasure of the next spectacle. The immediate delight in what is before her eyes at any particular moment is entirely sufficient for her. For her brother, the moment's joy is the base for somewhat fretful speculation on the nature of man. The pain of time passing seems a specially human sorrow; the hunger for permanence a specially human appetite.

A preoccupation with time is almost the common denominator of post-Renaissance poets. If Wordsworth's consciousness of time is to be worth a special study, one must show either that his time consciousness was not merely typical or that he made a highly individual use of it, or both. One can, I think, do both. David Perkins has said of Wordsworth, "No poet gives us a more vivid picture of the mind encountering and building up its world."[3] This is perhaps a too compact expression of what Wordsworth's best poetry does and needs a little expanding. The mind encounters a Newtonian universe "out there," but brings to it an imaginative force which builds up a new creation. Nevertheless, whatever transforming gleam the auxiliar light may shed on nature, the world, as A. E. Housman lamented, "is the old world yet"—and growing older. And this fact, that both man and the universe in which he dwells are imprisoned in time, constitutes for the post-Renaissance poet the very nature of man's apparently tragic plight. Now where Wordsworth seems to me to be so individual in his treatment of time is that for him it is not man's limitations but his unique gifts that are the source of his pain and fear. Those very powers that seem to hint that he is not entirely subject to process most sharply disturb him. The perception is not unique to Wordsworth. Burns had told his mouse that the tiny creature was blessed in being trapped in the present—the poet has to "guess and fear" the future. "We look before and after," complained Shelley, "and pine for what is not."

Memory and imagination seem to offer, not perhaps an escape from time, but a kind of circumscribed freedom within it. It is by memory and imagination that we perceive and measure time, and the human mind is a willful clock, as Virginia Woolf recognized.

> An hour, once it lodges in the queer element of the human spirit, may be stretched to fifty or a hundred times its clock length; on the other hand, an hour may be accurately represented on the timepiece of the mind by one second. This extraordinary discrepancy between time on the clock and time in the mind is less known than it should be and deserves fuller investigation.[4]

The vagaries of the mind's perception of time may, of course, be represented as an ability to see different kinds of time. Certainly there is in Wordsworth's work an implicit sense of different schemes of time, and in my examination of these I owe a great debt to the work of Herbert Lindenberger. In his book *On Wordsworth's "Prelude,"* he offers, not a detailed and comprehensive review of Wordsworth's time sense, but a remarkably stimulating and perceptive one. He notes Wordsworth's contrast of "inner" and "outer" time; outer time is clock and calendar time, while inner time is the time of memory and intuition, more readily responsive to nature's time than to clock time. He recognizes too Wordsworth's conception of two distinct realms, eternity and time, and points out that the poet's image of the former is rooted in this world. Finally, he places *The Prelude* in the "Time Book" tradition; in other words, he sees it as an essentially modern work which uses the exploration of time as a means of examining subjective experiences. The poem, says Lindenberger, attempts to confuse creatively the reader's ordinary sense of time and seeks to imitate, not the verifiable chronological order of events, but the structure of experience. In these ways it looks forward to the work of novelists such as George Eliot, Marcel Proust, and James Joyce.[5]

There is one important point, however, on which I disagree with Lindenberger. As one reads his chapters, one is constantly aware of modes of time arranged in pairs: time and eternity, inner and outer time, the time of the incident and the time of writing, and so on. I agree with the definitions of, and distinctions between, these kinds of time; I do not accept that they can be simply paired off. There is in Wordsworth's time schemes a distinguishable, qualitative order. Thus the lowest time is clock time, mechanical in the narrowest sense, inflexible and uncreative. Next there is nature's time, Newtonian, a mathematical continuum, and also inflexible, but less artificial than clock time and more conducive to spiritual well-being. Above these two is inner time, felt by the nerves and brain and lodged, as Woolf put it, "in the queer element of the human spirit." This time is liberating and creative. And there appear to be occasions when inner time obliterates not merely the two inferior schemes, but itself also, bringing the mind to a visionary moment, an eternal present where "we see into the life of things."

The whole Wordsworthian view of time is much more suggestive of an ordered structure than of a set of pairs; the movement of feeling is much more like a progress from stage to stage than it is like a fight. Lindenberger, unfortunately, seems ensnared by his own notion of opposed pairs and is thus able to say, "One can read the poem almost like a morality play, with both forces alternately triumphing in the battle which rages within the poet."[6] One can, certainly, but I doubt if one should. There is struggle in Wordsworth's mind and there is a struggle in the poem. But "struggle" is not synonymous with "battle"; the struggle in *The Prelude* is partly a struggle for definition and partly a struggle to go on, to ascend some height, not to overthrow some enemy. The world of outer time is not defeated by inner time, it is simply left behind—and all time schemes are finally left behind in the supreme moments of vision.

I have no wish to wrench a philosophy out of material we value as poetry; one must tread exceedingly carefully in any consideration of the nature of that "eternal present" which Wordsworth seems to achieve in his visionary experiences. There are times when the poet seems to regard it as the durationless "moment" in which the eternal mind dwells and which the mystic seems to share with God in his moments of exaltation. What Wordsworth believed or didn't believe is unimportant, however; it is the literary value of these moments that matters, and that value lies, I think, not in the description of eternity, but in the description of time apparently seen from that vantage point and in the manner in which that vantage point was gained.

Wordsworth's eternity is attained by a kind of spiritual or psychological ascent. His time schemes seem to constitute a kind of hierarchy, and he seems to regard the natural pro-

gress of the mind as upwards, through the hierarchy, to a
moment joined to eternity. The incidents leading to the great
moments of vision are always introduced casually, with reference to material time. The skating episode (*Prelude,* 1:425–
63) begins at six o'clock on a winter evening, and from this
point on we see Wordsworth defying all time scales. The
village clock strikes six; he ignores it, as he ignores the time
hints of the blazing cottage windows. But he defies nature's
time too. When the orange sky of evening dies away and the
stars eastward are sparkling clear, he goes on skating. He is
absorbed in inner time: "happy time / . . . for all of us, for
me / It was a time of rapture" (11:428–30). And by means of
this inner time, this "deliberate holiday," he is led to a moment outside the clock, as it were, where he can see time
proceeding—the earth rolling "with visible motion her diurnal round."

Although such moments seem to be outside time,
Wordsworth called them "spots of time" (*Prelude,* 12:208).
He did so, perhaps, because they appear to be "discrete"
moments in the sense that a philosopher might use that word.
They seem to be separate moments, unconnected with the
apparent flux of time before and after. In this respect at least,
Wordsworth's notion is analogous to Descartes's idea of the
separate moment, an idea that had in some ways dominated
seventeenth-century metaphysical thinking. Coupled with
the belief that God could and might choose to annihilate man
at any moment, the idea may well have added something to
the melancholy foreboding that characterized an age of yearly
plagues and continual wars. But although Wordsworth has
moods of deep pessimism, for him the discrete moment is
almost always an occasion of joy (as it had been for
Descartes), and on other occasions a moment of knowing or
recognition. It is never an occasion of despair.

My chief interest, in spite of the allusion to Descartes, is
not a search for origins. Nevertheless, I must glance briefly at
one set of notions about time and the mind which almost
certainly influenced Wordsworth: the psychological theory

of associationism. In the eighteenth century the Cartesian "moment of thought" had become a moment of sensation; man lived intensely in the moment, creating himself in his sensations and creating also a sense of duration by the memory of succeeding moments. Memory, of course, is stimulated by association. The notion of affective memory binding together disparate moments to form a sense of time elapsing requires the notion that one image seen or remembered will suggest other images with which it has been grouped in the past. Wordsworth uses associationism and affective memory so often and so noticeably that I need not illustrate the matter here; it will in any case be demonstrated over and over again in succeeding chapters. But we must look a little more closely at how Wordsworth came to be influenced by associationism, at some implications of the doctrine, and at what he took and what he rejected of it.

Melvin Rader's *Wordsworth, a Philosophical Approach* begins with evidence for how much time Wordsworth and others must have spent listening to Coleridge. Coleridge charmed all his listeners, but he did much more than charm Wordsworth. Moreover, as Rader points out, when Wordsworth met Coleridge in 1795 he was in a period of severe moral crisis and had "Yielded up moral questions in despair" (*Prelude,* 11:305). He was, therefore, peculiarly open to such an influence as Coleridge's. It is not unfair, nor particularly unkind either, to say that Wordsworth's verse suggests that his philosophical notions are derived from the conversations of a gifted friend rather than from systematic study. According to Rader, Coleridge greatly admired David Hartley (author of *Observations on Man* and founder of the associationist school of psychology) until 1801, when, after a serious illness, he announced that he had "overthrown" the doctrine of associationism. At about the same time, and apparently for similar reasons, he rejected necessitarianism, the doctrine that the associative process must inevitably take place and does not depend on the consent of the individual will. Coleridge had come to feel that the two doctrines represented "the

irreligious metaphysics of modern Infidels."[7] Having first by
his enthusiastic expositions persuaded Wordsworth to accept
these doctrines, Coleridge later persuaded him to reject them.

But something of both of these doctrines continued to
shape Wordsworth's thought. The characteristic Wordsworthian notion that a life lived in daily presence of natural
beauty must inevitably predispose the mind to serenity and
benevolence has implicit in it not merely the doctrines of
association and necessity, but also of perfectibility: if all men
could be exposed only to the most benevolent stimuli, mankind could be brought to a state of moral perfection. But one
implication of these doctrines Wordsworth certainly rejected.
Associationism and necessitarianism reduce the mind to
being a mere spectator of the universe, but Wordsworth insists on its creative power, on the interaction between the
mind and what it observes. What remains of associationism
in Wordsworth's mind is that element which is most useful
for his purposes as a poet. Denied the myths and gods of the
classical past, the Romantic poet must make his own efficacious symbols. If it is true that ideas or sensations experienced
together often and vividly will suggest each other when experienced individually, and if, furthermore, it is true that
associations tend to run into clusters and thus form complex
ideas and emotions, then the poet can form his own potent
symbols by the apposition of images drawn from the world
around him, by linking particular thoughts and feelings with
these groups of images, and by frequent repetition of the
image groups and the sensations and sentiments related to
them. This is the method of *The Prelude*.

But our chief interest in associationism is its relationship
to memory. Rader points out that the idea of associationism
did not originate with Hartley; Aristotle had described it and
explained memory in terms of associative links. Thomas
Hobbes, John Locke, and Bishop Berkeley note the necessity
of custom and repetition in the association of ideas.[8] Associationism thus met a need arising from eighteenth-century
deism. God having been pushed back to the beginning of

things, one could only create a sense of duration from the endless series of separate instants by associative memories. In doing this one also created a self: all those innumerable "I's" that existed in all those past, discrete moments became, in their interaction in memory, an "I" that seemed to endure. Through memory the "I" achieved that unceasing, uninterrupted being that Cartesian discontinuity, coupled with the preeminence of efficient second causes, had taken away. For Coleridge, the separate instant was not so much a frightening idea as a silly one.

> How opposite to nature and to fact to talk of the "one moment" of Hume, of our whole being an aggregate of single sensations! Who ever felt a single sensation? Is not everyone at the same moment conscious that there coexists a thousand others, a darker shade, or less light, even as when I fix my attention on a white house, or a grey bare hill, or rather long ridge that runs out of sight each way.... And what is a moment? Succession with interspace? Absurdity! It is evidently only the licht-punct in the indivisible undivided duration.[9]

Undoubtedly Wordsworth too was persuaded of the necessary truth of the "indivisible undivided duration." Nonetheless, his poetry operates so frequently and so powerfully by associative methods—the repetition of moments of insight to create a sense of self and the nature of self, and the linking of these moments by memory—that we must suppose the Hartleian residue in his consciousness was considerable. But it is as the basis of a poetic method, I think, that Wordsworth retained vestiges of associationism, rather than as a serious belief about the nature of the mind, and I shall say more about the form this takes in chapter 3.

Wordsworth's time consciousness, however, was something richer and subtler than any philosophical scheme he might have absorbed from Coleridge, and certainly richer than any scheme a reader may extrapolate from his work. Nevertheless, certain provisional distinctions help to identify what is happening in the poetry. A good deal of excellent spadework has already been done. Christopher Salvesen's *Landscape of Memory* (1965) has already become something of a classic, and I am particularly indebted for Salvesen's suggestion of the ways in which Wordsworth may have been influenced by Descartes. John Garetson Dings, in *The Mind in Its Place* (1973), argues that Wordsworth's search for something enduring is, particularly in the pastorals, a quest for "rootedness"—a quality he found in the life of the "statesmen" of the Lake District. E. L. Stelzig offers a refreshing corrective in *All Shades of Consciousness* (1975) to the still fashionable view of Wordsworth as a great Romantic stoic. Stelzig is particularly good on "Resolution and Independence"; he is courageous enough to say that he finds in the Leech-gatherer a "fuller humanization of the poet's imagination" than he does in the defeated Margaret of "The Ruined Cottage."[10] There is indeed more to Wordsworth's conception of the self in time than is suggested by weary platitudes about the human condition, and it is encouraging to find an able scholar who is willing to say so.

It seems to me, however, that the works of all of these men, however valuable they are, are commentaries rather than criticism; they work backwards from the texts to the thoughts, feelings, and circumstances of the poet. This is a daunting task; Wordsworth himself commented on the difficulty of deciding which part of the river of a man's mind comes from which fountain. My own task is no less daunting, but it is radically different. Rader, Salvesen, Dings, Stelzig, and Lindenberger endeavor to explain how the poet's words got onto the page; I want to show what the words do once they are there.

I do not propose, however, merely to ignore the matter of Wordsworth's ideas and beliefs; I shall find it necessary to examine what he seemed to assume on particular occasions about the nature of the mind and of time. The unique aspects of Wordsworth's time sense are, first, his constant awareness that the pain and fear with which man confronts time result not from the mind's limitations, but from its qualities; and second, his notions that all modes of sensing time are not equally valuable and that the mind can move from lower to higher time schemes. My scrutiny of Wordsworth's highly original treatment of these themes is the substance of this book, but it may be helpful to give a brief preliminary indication of the nature and scope of my examination. The purely literary value of Wordsworth's beliefs and perceptions lies in the poetic energy they generate. A great deal of this energy is produced by a predominant and almost unceasing conflict between the mind's hunger for immutability and its perception of an organic, changing, external universe. But more particular to Wordsworth is the energy generated by a paradox: the very powers that seem to point to the mind's independence also enable it to perceive that it is enmeshed in mortality. The energy generated in both of these ways is experienced by the reader as the stuff of literature; Wordsworth's sense of time is not merely a theme in his verse, it is a prevalent motif, a catalyst in the imagery, part of the manner in which the poetry works. Most notably and pervasively, the reader is stirred by the vitality of Wordsworth's time consciousness as the poet's sensibility moves from one time scheme to another. Serious students of Wordsworth have in the recent past been fortunate in a wealth of exploratory and exegetical scrutiny of the content and origins of the poet's work. What I am attempting now is to show why, in its true nature as poetry, that work continues to be worth reading. I am concerned with time and mind as images and motifs out of which the poetry is made.

Since I am mainly concerned with literary values, I have confined my attention largely, though not exclusively, to the greatest poetry in the best version available. Unfortunately, not everyone now agrees on what is best. I have chosen to base my discussion of *The Prelude* on the 1850 text, even though this choice will seem to many people to call for justification, and to provide such justification is not an easy task in the present climate of opinion. Fortunately, I am able to allow Ernest de Selincourt to conduct a large part of my case for me. In the introduction to his parallel texts edition, he says:

> No one would doubt that the 1850 version is a better compo-
> sition than the A text. Weak phrases are strengthened, and the
> whole composition is more closely knit. The A text leaves
> often the impression of a man writing rapidly, thinking aloud
> or talking to his friend without waiting to shape his thought
> into the most concise and telling form, satisfied for the mo-
> ment if he can put it into metre by inverting the prose order of
> the words.[11]

The only reason for preferring the 1805 version (and it is the
reason which is now always brought forth) is that the first
text represents the "authentic" Wordsworth of the great
decade—that is, it represents most truly his thought, philosophy, and moral views during that period of his life. This
reason will be sufficient for those who believe that the value
of literature lies chiefly in the clues it offers to the philosophy
and thoughts the author might be supposed to have entertained at the time of writing. But I suggest that readers value
poetry for its total effect on their sensibilities, and it is this
total effect by which we should measure which text we prefer. It ought to go without saying that poetry's capacity to
excite our sensibilities most fully is connected only in an
indirect and often minor way with the reducible thought
content which it can be shown to render.

I find it difficult to decide what view of literary value de
Selincourt held. Within a mere fifteen pages of the passage I
have just quoted, we find this:

> When his poetry was commended for the purity of its moral
> he insisted that he, on the other hand, valued it according to
> the powers of mind which it presupposed in the writer and
> excited in the hearer. That work of his which most trium-
> phantly stands this test belongs to the years 1798–1807.
>
> (P. lxxiv)

The last sentence is more than a non sequitur; it is a simple contradiction of what de Selincourt stated in the first sentence of the earlier passage. It is also, in fact, directly contrary to the sentence which immediately precedes it. De Selincourt seems to have misunderstood Wordsworth. The poet is not saying that unorthodox ideas are more exciting than "purity of moral," he is saying that great poetry is more exciting in its own nature than any doctrine it may be thought to contain; the "powers of mind" it presupposes in the author are his powers, not to formulate thought or assume feeling, but to express the full richness of experience as only great poetry can express it. To prefer, as de Selincourt does, the admittedly inferior poetry because of its supposed authenticity is to fall into the equal and opposite error to that of the moralists. What de Selincourt is saying seems to amount to this: "Of course everyone agrees that, judged by literary criteria, the 1850 version is better than the 1805; nevertheless, for other reasons we must now prefer the inferior composition."

This is not my preference, and evidently would not have been Wordsworth's. Neither, one may suppose, would it have been de Selincourt's if he had really understood the magnitude of the superiority of the 1850 version. Although he saw that the later text is better, he had no conception of how much better. The improvements seemed to him to be matters of tidying up, smoothing out, and fidgeting for aptness of diction. His comparison of the 1805 and 1850 versions of a famous passage from book 4 is typical of his analysis.

> Magnificent
> The morning was, a memorable pomp,
> More glorious than I ever had beheld.
> The Sea was laughing at a distance; all
> The solid Mountains were as bright as clouds.
> (1805, ll. 330–34)

> Magnificent
> The morning rose, in memorable pomp,
> Glorious as e'er I had beheld—in front,

The sea lay laughing at a distance; near,
The solid mountains shone, bright as the clouds.

(1850, ll. 323–27)

For de Selincourt, the revision involved substituting verbs of
more definite meaning for "was"; the improvement consisted in a "gain of strength and vividness" (p. lviii). He did
not see that the 1850 text creates powerful images where they
did not exist before. "The morning rose, in memorable
pomp" suggests the Sun King's splendid levee, and thereby
also by how much nature's commonplace events outdo the
most lavish human grandeur. He did not see that "The sea lay
laughing at a distance" is a true personification, suggesting a
kingly, destructively powerful but presently benevolent giant
taking his joyful ease; and he did not see that "The solid
mountains shone" contains an implicit oxymoron which
suggests a uniquely incandescent quality of morning light. It
was not Wordsworth's preference for more definite meaning
but his fuller grasp of the imagery that prompted the sub-
stitution of verbs. An exhaustive critical comparison of the
two texts would, I believe, demonstrate throughout the
superiority of the 1850 version.

It is also necessary to defend my use of *The Excursion,*
book 1, for my discussion of "The Ruined Cottage." The
chief concern of Jonathan Wordsworth's *Music of Humanity*
(1960) is to promulgate the MS D text of "The Ruined Cottage," in which the story of Margaret is separated from the
life history of the Pedlar. In MS E, the standard text of book
1 of *The Excursion,* the two elements are united again.
Jonathan Wordsworth prefers D on the grounds that the
story of Margaret and the biography of the Pedlar are poetry
of radically different kinds and that the first gains nothing
from union with the second. Paul D. Sheats has already given
a full and sensitive account of what readers gain from a
knowledge of the Pedlar's history, and I will not do an injustice to his commentary by trying to make a précis of it here.[12]
All I need to say now is that the Pedlar is an involved narrator

of Margaret's story, and we need to know something of the formation and habits of the compassionate and judicious mind through which the main parts of the story come to us. For Jonathan Wordsworth, the greatness of Margaret's story is in the tender love for a suffering person which it manifests; I agree, but the expression of such love is enriched, not baffled, by the criticism implicit in the manner in which the details of the story are revealed, and by the subtlety which discriminates, also implicitly, between catastrophe and tragedy. I hope that I make these matters clear in chapter 4.

MS D is, says Jonathan Wordsworth, "essentially a rationalisation of work on 'The Ruined Cottage' up to and including March 1798," and he offers it as "the best balanced and most coherent surviving version" of Margaret's story. "The later history of the poem is one of odd local improvements and general deterioration." The "local improvements" seem to me to add up to something very substantial, but to examine them here would be too large a digression. As for the "general deterioration," Jonathan Wordsworth makes a valid point in identifying it with the poet's habit of making comment and judgment unnecessarily explicit, of "forcing his implications into the open."[13] But there seems to be very little of this in the standard text, and I suspect that Jonathan Wordsworth sees more than is really there because he is influenced by extraliterary considerations.

Jonathan Wordsworth's final summation of his argument for MS D supports my suspicion. Commenting on Wordsworth's 1845 revision of the poem to insert an orthodox religious reflection at the end of the Pedlar's narrative, he says:

> However, the reason why Margaret lives on so long is not "the unbounded might of prayer," but the "torturing hope" that Robert will come back. With Matthew—
> I look'd at her, and look'd again
> —And did not wish her mine
> —and Leonard of *The Brothers,* and Michael, she exists to show that the Wordsworth of 1797–1800 did not believe in a

consolation springing "From sources deeper far than deepest pain." Her story must now be read not as Wordsworth left it at the age of 75, but as it stood nearly 50 years before, at the end of the eighteenth century.[14]

This passage reads like an elliptical syllogism in which the major assumption has been left out. The author not only assumes his first premise, but assumes our concurrence. Although the last sentence is not introduced by the argumentative conjunction, one cannot avoid reading the passage as saying, "MS D belongs to the period when Wordsworth did not believe in a deep source of consolation, and therefore we must prefer D to E." My objection is not merely that the syllogism lacks a clearly stated major premise, but that it implies a philosophic rather than a literary preference.

One really must try to see a piece of literature as in itself it really is. Margaret does not exist to show what Wordsworth didn't believe at the time; she exists for a host of more complex and more important reasons. Poetry itself does not exist to show what the poet believed or didn't believe (though it may reflect these matters); it exists to show the powers of mind which may be presumed in the author and to excite the capacities of the reader. It is a naive and potentially corrupting mistake to suppose otherwise.

2

Ordered and Disordered Time

We must now scrutinize more carefully Wordsworth's characteristic methods of indicating time and its passing, since these methods reveal the manner in which he sensed time and therefore the manner in which he wished his readers to sense it. He does, of course, often use conventional terms: "The village clock struck six," "the stroke of nine," "Five years have passed," and so on. But for his more serious purposes, it would seem, as Lindenberger puts it, that "the calendar and, indeed, all publicly measurable units of time come to seem crudely inadequate."[1] More often and more effectively, he uses the natural situation to identify a moment or measure duration. All the same, we know that we could make a reasonable guess at what the clocks and calendars would say at such moments, and it is this submerged awareness of conventional time that enriches such imagery. The point has been well made by Geoffrey Durrant.

In Wordsworth the sense of an ordered common time is almost always conveyed. This is not to assert that Wordsworth

gives a precise hour and date for the experiences recorded, but
that he conveys the sense that the event could be so recorded if
necessary. As in his ordering of sense experience Wordsworth
retains the spatial structure of the objective world, so in his
treatment of subjective experience he retains always the sense
of an objective measurable time to which it can be related.
These are, I believe, important sources of the firmness, clar-
ity, and solidity of his world.[2]

In nearly all the passages which I shall discuss in this chapter,
the element which invigorates the poetry is the time scheme
which has ostensibly been left behind, the unseen clock. In
book 6 of *The Prelude,* for instance, we are told that part of
the Alpine peasant's peace of mind is his habitual response to
natural stimuli, rather than to, for example, the chiming of a
clock. Wordsworth sees him as

> Contented, from the moment that the dawn
> (Ah! surely not without attendant gleams
> Of soul-illumination) calls him forth
> To industry, by glistenings flung on rocks,
> Whose evening shadows lead him to repose.
>
> (Ll. 512–16)

Two things distinguish these lines from minor landscape
verse: first, the careful placing of "gleams," which encourages us to interpret it literally for an instant, before the
metaphorical sense is made obvious; second, the economy of
"glistenings," implying rain or dew on the rocks on which
the early sun is shining. Wordsworth's use of sun, moon,
stars, earth, and atmosphere to measure time or specify a
moment has a sharp focus that makes it quite different from
imagery produced by literary habit. Note, for example, the
accuracy of the following lines from book 8:

>   A diamond light
> (Whene'er the summer sun, declining, smote
> A smooth rock wet with constant springs) was seen

Sparkling from out a copse-clad bank that rose
Fronting our cottage.

(Ll. 406–10)

We are made to see what is really, unexpectedly, there; our
eyes are directed to the particular spot from where the light of
the declining sun rebounds with such surprising flashes.
"Diamond" and "sparkling" suggest a hard glitter of light in
contrast to conventional notions of evening light, when
"barred clouds bloom the soft-dying day."

While accuracy of this kind reveals an authentic poet, it
is in itself straightforward and carries no load heavier than
description. We must now examine another sort of exactitude—more complex, functionally more important, and
purposefully hidden in apparent vagueness. In book 2 of *The
Prelude,* the poet says that as

a boy I loved the sun,
Not as I since have loved him, as a pledge
And surety of our earthly life, a light
Which we behold and feel we are alive;
Nor for his bounty to so many worlds—
But for this cause, that I had seen him lay
His beauty on the morning hills, had seen
The western mountain touch his setting orb,
In many a thoughtless hour, when, from excess
Of happiness, my blood appeared to flow
For its own pleasure.

(Ll. 178–88)

The whole scene is a sundial: morning casts brightness on the
hills; evening throws them into silhouette. But sundials do
not tell the time, people do, and human consciousness of time
and moment is modified by an endless variety of moods.
Wordsworth is not ensnared in Newton's absolute space-
time, even though his time consciousness is that of a man
who has grasped the notion of a continuum. He never
specifies the time merely for the sake of doing so; the hour,

the place, and the feeling are all of a piece. It is a time-space-mind continuum. In *The Prelude,* 2:183–86, this wholeness is conveyed by a syntactical trick that at first looks merely slipshod.

> I had seen him lay
> His beauty on the morning hills, had seen
> The western mountain touch his setting orb,
> In many a thoughtless hour...

Which of the verbs is modified by the adverbial clause? By the time common sense has construed it with the repeated "seen," the initial reading prompted by juxtaposition has attributed the thoughtless mood to the sun and mountains. An insistence on absolute space-time would have none of this; the mood of intuitive joy would be seen as Wordsworth's only, irrelevant to the strict registration of spatial dispositions. But for Wordsworth the time-space arrangement includes his mind and its moods. Human time is finally the only time that matters, and Wordsworth has made this point by allowing us to recognize, in a moment of apparent confusion, that sun and mountains really are "thoughtless."

Once one acknowledges human consciousness as an integral element of space-time, the whole matter is transposed from a mathematical to a poetic affair. It is not merely that human observation is at all times modified or distorted by nervous and emotional sensibility; the human mind has a penchant for remembering and counting. Consciousness, therefore, can set against the repetitive planetary motions a straight-line motion of progress or decay.

> 'Twas not indifferent to a youthful mind
> To mark some sheltering bower or sunny nook,
> Where an old man had used to sit alone,
> Now vacant; pale-faced babes whom I had left
> In arms, now rosy prattlers at the feet
> Of a pleased grandame tottering up and down;
> And growing girls whose beauty, filched away

With all its pleasant promises, was gone
To deck some slighted playmate's homely cheek.

(Prelude, 4:200–208)

In spite of passages like this, Bernard Blackstone complains that there is no real counterpoint of cyclic and progressive patterns. "Wordsworth's journey ... can hardly be called a journey at all: his course is circular, and his paradise is a mountain valley." A few pages later he continues: "Wordsworthian Wanderers move in circles; they are assimilated, that is, to planetary rather than to human patterns. This poetry forms a natural bridge between the human and the cosmic travellers. There is no progression. Wordsworth is caught within his 'cirque' of hills and resists dislodgement."[3]

Blackstone implies that Wordsworth takes refuge in the planetary motion, conjuring a spurious sense of invulnerability to time from the repeated alterations of seasons and star systems. But the human mind remembers and counts and does not confuse similarity with sameness. Identical twins are not one person, and although this day may be exactly like a certain day many years ago, it is not the same day. People grow older, and things are different. The unseen clock is still moving. Wordsworth makes the point clearly enough in "The Two April Mornings."

We walked along, while bright and red
Uprose the morning sun;
And Matthew stopped, he looked, and said,
'The will of God be done!'

(Ll. 1–4)

The sun is the time reference, fixing the moment not as an entry in a diary or a date in a biography, but in order fully to represent the anagnorisis and self-knowing of which the moment is an essential element. Perhaps not every reader will immediately connect Matthew's exclamation with the sun's rising, though a hint is given in "he looked and said" and is repeated with emphasis in the fourth stanza.

> 'what thought,
> Beneath so beautiful a sun,
> So sad a sigh has brought?'

(Ll. 14–16)

When Matthew replies, "fixing still his eye / Upon the eastern mountain top" (ll. 18–19), the point is inescapable.

The space-time moment, the feeling, and the mental act are not merely strongly associated but integrated. The experience would not be impoverished by withdrawing one element; rather, it would not happen at all. Matthew recognizes the moment as an exact replica of one thirty years ago. The similarity is emphasized by his stopping a second time and noting the detail of the cloud's "long purple cleft." It is not merely the same time of day and the same sort of day. The whole situation is in detail the same.

> 'And just above yon slope of corn
> Such colours, and no other,
> Were in the sky, that April morn,
> Of this the very brother.'

(Ll. 25–28)

Thus it is the consciousness of repetition, rather than mere memory, that the poem is dealing with. Emma's death did not take place on the first April morning; the point now reiterated—the finality of loss despite time's apparent cyclical renewals—was first perceived as Matthew stopped short by his daughter's grave. What he perceived was the uniqueness of each human person and the special uniqueness of kinship. He is gladdened by the beauty of the child he meets beside the churchyard yew, but "I looked at her, and looked again / And did not wish her mine!" (ll. 55–56). His dead daughter is irreplaceable.

In like manner, the affinity he now feels between himself and his young pupil is not kinship and cannot be. The repetition of the space-time situation therefore has an approximate parallel in the human situation. Matthew is with a younger person whom he admires or likes but who cannot replace what he has lost. But the differences in the human situation—thirty years ago the chance-met, beautiful child, now the young man, his pupil—are more important than the similarity. Because the human situation is different, the total situation is different, no matter how exactly the spatial relationships are repeated. The repetitions can be counted—thirty years have passed. Times have changed; there is no immunity in the "cyclic temporal patterns";[4] people die, and they are irreplaceable.

The pain of man's ability to remember but not recover the past is expressed even more explicitly in "The Fountain."

> We talked with open heart, and tongue
> Affectionate and true,
> A pair of friends, though I was young,
> And Matthew seventy-two.

> (Ll. 1–4)

The difference in age is important: it suggests that the Wordsworth who speaks in the poem is young enough to be Matthew's son; it is evidence of an unusually strong affinity between the two men; and it is part of the sense of a disturbed time consciousness which becomes explicit in the references to the "crazy old church clock." Wordsworth's proposal that they should match the fountain's music with human song, in particular with Matthew's half-mad witty song about the "bewildered chimes," is a means of emphasizing time contrasts. The music of the waters, for Matthew, celebrates permanence, freedom from grief and the fear of death.

> 'No check, no stay, this Streamlet fears;
> How merrily it goes!
> 'Twill murmur on a thousand years,
> And flow as now it flows.'

> (Ll. 21–24)

By contrast, Matthew's own habitual merriment has a sense
of strain; it is a matter of will rather than condition, for he is
the "grey-haired man of glee." His old man's eyes are filled
with "childish" tears, for he has grown from child to man,
and yet "the same sound is in my ears / Which in those days I
heard" (ll. 31–32). The stream fulfills the same purpose as the
circling planets in suggesting that time is not totally destruc-
tive, but the apparent immutability of such natural objects
offers no illusion. On the contrary, it intensifies man's painful consciousness of his own straight-time path to the grave.
(Here surely is the counterpoint Blackstone is seeking.)

The whole of "The Fountain" is deceptively worked
out, the simple diction and meter constantly encouraging us
to anticipate equally simple observations and comments, and
we come upon the real meaning with a mild shock of surprise. We assume that Matthew is mourning his lost youth,
but he is not. He grieves for what he retains. His consciousness appears to be unaffected by age; the same sound is in his
ears which he heard as a vigorous young man. Other living
creatures are spared the specially human suffering of a mind
whose perceptions seem immune from change but which is
lodged in a changing body. The blackbird and the lark are
happier than man, not because they are free, but because they
are bound by natural laws. As Matthew says: "With Nature
never do *they* wage / A foolish strife" (ll. 41–42). But man,
by virtue of his self-consciousness, has a certain painful independence of the natural time cycle. He can remember lost joy
and perceive in his deprivation objects associated with his lost
happiness. Worse, he is bound by social laws and moral
habits, laws heavier than nature's. The natural world knows
nothing of determined cheerfulness.

The specially human pain, however, arises from the
specially human superiority—the independent mind with its
self-reflecting self-consciousness. Such a mind is capable of
protest, of wishing the natural time process to be reversible
while knowing that it is not. And such a mind is capable of
expressing the wish and the protest in a mood of self-
mocking gaiety.

And, ere we came to Leonard's rock,
He sang those witty rhymes
About the crazy old church-clock,
And the bewildered chimes.

(Ll. 69–72)

Wordsworth's continuum, then, differs from Newton's in that it includes the mind of the observer. The mind, however, differs from the other elements in the continuum in that it can do what sun and moon cannot. It can remember, and, to a very large extent, choose what to remember. Man can think back, but he cannot turn time back; his independence, though not spurious, is partial. This partial independence is inescapably painful, and one of the consequences is a disorder in our consciousness of time.

I now wish to consider briefly two sources of this sense of disorder. Urban man, living within temperate northern latitudes, has come to have certain expectations about darkness and light. He expects night to fall at a certain time, subject to seasonal variations, and he expects to become aware of the moon, if the moon is up, during a certain period. Habitually, if not entirely consciously, he relates these expectations about natural time to clock time and the calendar, and if this relationship seems to be disturbed, he may be disconcerted and frightened. Eclipses are now part of our scheme of expectations, but an unpredicted dust storm darkening a city can still produce nervous shivers. The sense of menace which people often feel during such happenings is perhaps one of the things Arthur Koestler is exploiting in his title *Darkness at Noon*.

Another assumption about time so basic and necessary to man that it is now a subject of government statistics and bureaucratic terminology is "expectation of life." In spite of the unavoidable knowledge of human vulnerability, people nearly always describe themselves as shocked by news of an early death, and obituaries almost always use the word "untimely." Man's most bewildered grief is for his dead children, and the bewilderment consists in the powerful sense

that death has come before it should. One of the effects of this
almost universal conviction that the passing of a child is untimely is difficulty in grasping the fact of such a death.
Wordsworth certainly experienced difficulty in realizing his
own daughter's death, as he records in what I consider to be
his greatest sonnet.

> Surprised by joy—impatient as the Wind
> I turned to share the transport—Oh! with whom
> But Thee, deep buried in the silent tomb.
>
> (*P.W.*, 3:16)

The poem goes on to ask, "But how could I forget thee?"
The answer may be simply that in reality he didn't forget her;
the astonishing truth which the poem celebrates is that he had
forgotten that she was dead.

The two senses of disordered time that I have just described, darkness at noon and early death, are brought together with superb effect in "Lucy Gray." Notice the chilling
suggestions of untimely darkness in lines 13–20.

> 'To-night will be a stormy night—
> You to the town must go;
> And take a lantern, Child, to light
> Your mother through the snow.'
>
> 'That, Father! will I gladly do:
> 'Tis scarcely afternoon—
> The minster-clock has just struck two,
> And yonder is the moon!'

The effect is "analogous to the supernatural."[5] Time is, apparently, ominously accelerating; the human time convention (the minster-clock) is outpaced by the hurrying universal
symbols. (Coleridge achieves the same premonitory chill in
The Ancient Mariner: "The sun's rim dips, the stars rush
out, / At one stride comes the dark.") The reader senses that
the parents' searching must be vain. By the social calendar

Lucy is a child, but by the calendar of natural circumstances she is on the brink of death—"The storm came on before its time" (1. 29).

But lines 13–20 do not merely cast their shadow over what follows. When we read the poem again, the first stanza also is tinged with numinous suggestions.

> Oft I had heard of Lucy Gray:
> And, when I crossed the wild,
> I chanced to see at break of day
> The solitary child.

A child alone at daybreak and "in the wild" is an alarming and piteous sight in itself, but a second reading detects the sense that Lucy is a ghost, one of Wordsworth's eternal wanderers. This sense has its origin in the supernatural fear aroused by the time images in dramatic juxtaposition: "The minster-clock has just struck two, / And yonder is the moon!"

The moon has a very similar function in "Strange fits of passion." The immediate effect of this poem—sharp and irrational apprehension—is again achieved by making time appear to accelerate. The illusion which gives rise to this effect has an importance which I will attend to later; for the moment all that needs to be said is that the poem is not weakened by the fact that it is an illusion. The real point of the poem is a jarring disturbance of that complacent mood in which a lover feels that he and his beloved are isolated from natural circumstances, and so from time.

> In one of those sweet dreams I slept,
> Kind Nature's gentlest boon!
> And all the while my eyes I kept
> On the descending moon.
>
> (Ll. 17–20)

The "sweet dream" is a blissful sense of invulnerability, which, though illusory, is one of nature's blessings. The lover, like the healthy child, feels his life in every limb; accident and the possibility of death can hardly seem real to him. But it is perhaps part of nature's ministry of fear (see *Prelude,* 1:301–2, 351–56) that, having given this mood to the young, she pierces it with freezing apprehensions.

David Perkins has said, "A romantic poem especially exploits and depends on our sense of time passing. . . . Often, in fact, it exhibits the drama of a man discovering his meaning."[6] In "Strange fits of passion," the poet's manipulation of the reader's sense of time is used first to establish the complacent mood and then to destroy it. The symbol of time is, of course, "moon," shamelessly rhymed with "June" (l. 6) for the enduring clichés ("Fresh as a rose" [1. 6] and "I to her cottage bent my way" [1. 7]) are precisely the means to indicate the slumbrous complacency of mutual love. The repetition of "moon" (five times in twenty-one lines) is conscious and purposeful; the tension of the poem is developed by insisting on the same symbol while adroitly changing the mood symbolized. The evening moon is a lovers' moon, and, as it hangs over the wide lea with no clouds to frame it, its travelling is unperceived. Thus it symbolizes, not merely the glamor of love, but love's spurious sense of timelessness.

The first hint of change is the quickening pace of the horse (ll. 11–12), indicating both the impatience of the lover and the alteration of horizon which will so frighteningly change the nature of the symbolism. As the lover approaches the cottage, the moon is first "sinking," then "descending," until finally, with dumbfounding speed, "down behind the cottage roof / At once the bright moon dropped" (ll. 23–24). And once more, at one stride comes the dark.

> What fond and wayward thoughts will slide
> Into a Lover's head!
> 'O mercy!' to myself I cried,
> 'If Lucy should be dead!'

                                                    (Ll. 25–28)

What has happened here is that the lover has made the mistake of attributing his own quickening pace to the moon and so misreads the symbol. The consequence is his irrational apprehension of Lucy's untimely death—the whole implication is that the lover reads this omen into the apparently unnatural acceleration of the setting moon. For him the planetary clocks have gone wild, and he experiences a rush of superstitious fear. And yet, one must reflect, not entirely superstitious after all. The lovers' moon really will set in a few hours' time, and sooner or later Lucy must die. The lover has in his irrational panic grasped the truth of the matter. The famous canceled stanza therefore had to be canceled.

> I told her this: her laughter light
> Is ringing in my ears:
> And when I think upon that night
> My eyes are dim with tears.
>
> (*P.W.*, 2:29n)

If allowed to stand, these lines would have misdirected the reader. Wordsworth has, as Perkins says, discovered his meaning: the substance of the lover's fear is not the possibility of untimely death but the certainty of ultimate death. Again we must admire the deceptive craft of a poem which is, as Geoffrey Durrant says, "a subtly worked out account of the relationship between man's inadequate sense of time, at the mercy of his hopes and illusions, and the absolute movement of the earth and of the planets which is the 'everlasting stream' upon which life is borne away."[7]

The notion that getting the time references wrong is a terrifying business is dealt with at length in *The Prelude,* 6:688–726, where Wordsworth describes the miserable night he spent with his college friend, Robert Jones, on their journey across the Alps. After two "golden days" beside Lake Como, the travellers were awakened in the middle of the night by the sound of a church clock. Misled by the chimes, they rose and resumed their journey by moonlight, thinking

that dawn must soon come and that they would enjoy a
prospect of the lake "Hushed in profound repose" (l. 699).
Soon they were lost and sat down on a rock to wait for
daylight (ll. 704–7). But it seemed daylight would never
come.

> From hour to hour
> We sate and sate, wondering, as if the night
> Had been ensnared by witchcraft. On the rock
> At last we stretched our weary limbs for sleep,
> But *could not* sleep, tormented by the stings
> Of insects, which, with noise like that of noon,
> Filled all the woods; the cry of unknown birds;
> The mountains more by blackness visible
> And their own size, than any outward light;
> The breathless wilderness of clouds; the clock
> That told, with unintelligible voice,
> The widely parted hours; the noise of streams,
> And sometimes rustling motions nigh at hand,
> That did not leave us free from personal fear;
> And, lastly, the withdrawing moon, that set
> Before us, while she still was high in heaven;—
> These were our food; and such a summer's night
> Followed that pair of golden days that shed
> On Como's Lake, and all that round it lay,
> Their fairest, softest, happiest influence.
>
> (6:707–26)

The prominent moon imagery links the whole passage with
"Lucy Gray" and "Strange fits of passion," and particularly
with the latter by virtue of the importance attached to the
unusual setting of the moon. Nevertheless, the confusion
here described is distinguished from other "mistakes" about
time in Wordsworth's verse in two ways: first, it is prolonged, whereas other examples are of momentary errors;
second, all the available schemes of time measurement are
misinterpreted, whereas in other cases only one mode is
wrongly understood. The result is a growing sense of alarm

as Wordsworth looks in turn at every set of time measures
and is baffled by all.

The imagery reflects increasing disturbance and dismay
as he continues his vain search for a recognizable time landmark. At first the church clock is alluded to neutrally; the
reader is simply told that Wordsworth and Jones did not
know its chiming code (ll. 693–4). The moonlight similarly
is simply named without epithet or qualifying phrase (l. 695).
At this stage, Wordsworth and Jones are mistaken but do not
know it. Their recognition of their time error comes slowly,
in the manner in which a traveller realizes he has lost his way.
Jones and Wordsworth are adrift both in space and time—
"lost, bewildered among woods immense" (l. 701). Thus
natural objects seem unnatural. The moon is reflected in a
lake of "sullen water" (l. 704) and is unlike the moon we have
seen in other poems. The brightness and fixed outlines have
gone; it is dull red and changes its form like a snake. The
mere fact that it is seen as a wavering reflection, not directly,
symbolizes the loss of a familiar and reliable time scheme.
Hence the now familiar twinge of half-superstitious fear:
"wondering as if the night / Had been ensnared by witch-
craft." Even the insects mislead the travellers "with noise like
that of noon," and the birds, being unknown, afford no time
clues with their cries. Nature, who, when her habits and
signals are known, seems to be fundamentally benevolent,
now seems malignantly careful to perplex, and the Wordsworthian heaven of Lake Como now has echoes of the
Miltonic hell: "The mountains more by blackness visible /
And their own size, than any outward light" (ll. 714–15).

When the clock is heard again, its sounds are unintelli-
gible. The hours it records are "widely parted"; civil time,
natural time, and sidereal time seem to be conspiring in an
evil hoax. The moon, already distorted by the sullen water,
moves in an unfamiliar plane: it is not setting but withdrawing, and this horizontal disappearance occurs while the moon
is still high in the heavens. But of course the travellers know
that the real moon is not set, just as they know that the clock

is not crazy like the church clock in "The Fountain," with its "bewildered chimes." And yet, as far as they are concerned, the clock might as well be crazy. There is a serious irony here, and its implication should not be overlooked. When Wordsworth comes across a clock whose chimes really do bewilder him, the effect is neither liberating nor reassuring.

Being thus lost in time is frightening in the same way as being lost in the ordinary way—a traveller becomes anxious only when he knows he is lost. A child or a half-wit could wander far away from familiar paths and fortuitously wander home again without having been disturbed for a moment. In such wandering, in fact, there may be a kind of transcendent joy, as in the following:

> For while they all were travelling home,
> Cried Betty, 'Tell us, Johnny, do,
> Where all this long night you have been,
> What you have heard, what you have seen:
> And, Johnny, mind you tell us true.'
>
> Now Johnny all night long had heard
> The owls in tuneful concert strive;
> No doubt too he the moon had seen;
> For in the moonlight he had been
> From eight o'clock till five.
>
> And thus, to Betty's question, he
> Made answer, like a traveller bold,
> (His very words I give to you,)
> 'The cocks did crow to-whoo, to-whoo,
> And the sun did shine so cold!'
> —Thus answered Johnny in his glory,
> And that was all his travel's story.
>
> ("The Idiot Boy," ll. 437–53)

Wordsworth and Jones were distressed because they knew they could not read any of the available clocks; the Idiot Boy never realized his misconceptions. It is the narrator who can measure the interval from eight o'clock till five; Johnny can't, and he spends these hours "in his glory." But what exactly does Wordsworth mean by this last phrase? It may be simply a way of describing Johnny's lunatic joy in his ride—his "glory" may be simply delight in seeing what he thinks are familiar objects in excitingly different guises. Such a view might adequately explain Johnny's glee, but it hardly explains the poet's. Not many people can have enjoyed reading "The Idiot Boy" as much as Wordsworth, according to his note on the poem, enjoyed writing it.

> The last stanza—"The Cocks did crow to-whoo, to-whoo, / And the sun did shine so cold"—was the foundation of the whole. The words are reported to me by my dear friend Thomas Poole; but I have heard the same repeated of other idiots. Let me add that this long poem was composed in the groves of Alfoxden, almost extempore; not a word, I believe, being corrected, though one stanza was omitted. I mention this in gratitude to those happy moments, for, in truth, I never wrote anything with so much glee.
>
> (*P.W.*, 2:478)

This passage expresses something different from Wordsworth's habit of overestimating his less successful work. Why such glee? The very word recalls Johnny's glory. The gibe that Wordsworth is himself the hero of the poem may find some justification, for Thomas Poole's anecdote seems to have aroused in Wordsworth the ecstatic liberation he attributes to Johnny. To be as much of an idiot as Johnny is to be free of time and its distresses; the owls and the moon are merely the familiar cocks and sun delightfully changed. Wordsworth's glee is possibly the joy of surrender to the wish that things were otherwise, that the mind was not conscious of the significance of temporal change. At the same time, the vehicle in which the wish is embodied is the adventure of an idiot—a recognition, probably, of what such surrender involves.

It may now seem that some of Blackstone's implications in phrases such as "his paradise is a mountain valley," and

"Wordsworth is caught within his 'cirque' of hills and resists dislodgement" are justifiable. Wordsworth feels the tug of escape and occasionally follows it. But this impulse does not show itself in the form of planetary motion; on the contrary, the illusion of timelessness depends upon the stars being obscured. The cloudless night sky is the most comprehensive reminder of man's imprisonment within the continuum; it is clock, calendar, map, and compass. When Wordsworth escapes from time, therefore, he escapes to a "secret place" (see "Three years she grew," ll. 25–30) where the universal symbols of time cannot be seen.

> I could record with no reluctant voice
> The woods of autumn, and their hazel bowers
> With milk-white clusters hung; the rod and line,
> True symbol of hope's foolishness, whose strong
> And unreproved enchantment led us on
> By rocks and pools shut out from every star,
> All the green summer, to forlorn cascades
> Among the windings hid of mountain brook.
>
> (*Prelude*, 1:483–90)

It seems likely that the fishing trip soon turned into a general exploration of the woods, and it was this leisurely rambling that exerted the "strong and unreproved enchantment." And when the grown man remembers the expedition as material for poetry, its nature changes again, and the enchantment that memory exerts is different from that of the experience itself. To see what this might be, one may look at the antithesis hidden in "shut out from every star / All the green summer." A contrast of night and day ("star" and "green") is suggested and thereby a natural time sequence. But the rocks and pools, being "shut out from every star," are shut out from the universal clocks. They are also, by the implications of "green summer," almost shut out from daylight. Outside the hazel bower is a world of alteration; within it are enchanting darkness and coolness, where the effects of time are not easily perceived.

The idea of a place so secluded that it suspends one's consciousness of time is explored further in "Nutting."

> O'er path-less rocks,
> Through beds of matted fern, and tangled thickets,
> Forcing my way, I came to one dear nook
> Unvisited, where not a broken bough
> Drooped with its withered leaves, ungracious sign
> Of devastation; but the hazels rose
> Tall and erect, with tempting clusters hung,
> A virgin scene!...
>
>   . . . . .
> Perhaps it was a bower beneath whose leaves
> The violets of five seasons re-appear
> And fade, unseen by any human eye;
> Where fairy water-breaks do murmur on
> For ever...
>
>   (Ll. 14–21, 30–34)

The stars are not mentioned in this poem, but the "beds of matted fern, and tangled thickets" through which Wordsworth has to force his way leave no doubt that what he finds is a "secret place." Plainly it is loved immediately as such— "dear nook / Unvisited" is a very potent antithesis. And until Wordsworth's violence, it was unravaged; no leaves were withered, no injured boughs drooped, the time-telling sky did not intrude. The timelessness of the place is also paradoxically suggested by the invasion of the human presence. Until that invasion, no human eye can count the violets' return. I have already noted that for Wordsworth human consciousness of time is paramount; if there is no mind to observe the scene, there is a kind of eternity in it. Wordsworth has come upon a timeless spot of earth, the contemplation of which enchants him almost as much as those supremely important durationless "spots of time." But the place loses this character as soon as it is seen; Wordsworth, being human, carries his time consciousness with him; the virgin scene is already raped by the eye that sees and the consciousness that counts.

The outrage that follows is perhaps a symbolic reenact-
ment of something that has already happened, though of
course the sexual connotations are clear and numerous
enough. Wordsworth's first emotion in his bower of bliss is
at least analogous to the erotic. The scene is "virgin," the
clusters are "tempting," and the hazels "rose erect."
Wordsworth responds with the confident tumescence of a
rapist who sees beauty naked and defenseless.

> A little while I stood,
> Breathing with such suppression of the heart
> As joy delights in; and, with wise restraint
> Voluptuous, fearless of a rival, eyed
> The banquet . . .
>
> (Ll. 21–25)

There is a luxurious, gloating pause. But between the volup-
tuary's appraising pause and the eventual rape, a curious
interval occurs. The ravisher's lustful mood changes to

> that sweet mood when pleasure loves to pay
> Tribute to ease; and, of its joy secure,
> The heart luxuriates with indifferent things,
> Wasting its kindliness on stocks and stones,
> And on the vacant air.
>
> (Ll. 39–43)

The rapist has forgotten about the rape, and the boy has
forgotten about collecting nuts. Wordsworth takes time off
from his intended business, plays with the flowers, lies down
beside the stream, and listens to the noise of its waters. Eventually, of course, he remembers what he came for, springs
up, and carries out his purpose with brutal vigor. We have a
very complex piece of verse here, and no doubt the tumescence, subsequent rape, and final remorse comprise the major
experience celebrated in the poem. But there is also a more
delicate experience: the strange intervening mood, the inex-

plicable suspension of predatory energy. Basically it is a mood of idleness, deliberate and blissful. The association of idleness, happiness, and timelessness is one which will become increasingly important in my examination of Wordsworth's time sense, and I will need to examine it in detail in a later chapter.

The secret places I have just been considering suggest timelessness in that they evoke a sense of isolation from the great natural clock, the massive cosmic time scheme of earth, sun, moon, and stars. In "The Two April Mornings" and "The Fountain," man's capacity to remember his lost joy and count his mortal years was seen as a kind of independence. But such independence is painful, because it is limited. Man is in truth part of the great clock, a fact which he is forced to remember when he is bereaved.

> A slumber did my spirit seal;
>   I had no human fears:
> She seemed a thing that could not feel
>   The touch of earthly years.
>
> No motion has she now, no force;
>   She neither hears nor sees;
> Rolled round in earth's diurnal course,
>   With rocks, and stones, and trees.
>
> (*P.W.*, 2:216)

Pessimism is neither so rare nor so pervasive in Wordsworth's poetry as critics with opposing views have claimed. But certainly it is expressed with unpretentious bleakness in this poem, which is most distinguished from its companion pieces in the Lucy series by an intuition, implicit throughout but breaking the surface of plain statement in the leaden word "diurnal," that the special glory of being alive and human is man's unique relationship to time. While we are alive we can walk towards the sun, and "Stepping westwards seems to be / A kind of *heavenly* destiny" ("Stepping

Westward," *P.W.*, 3:76, ll. 11–12). But only while we are
alive. Lucy dead has no power of her own; she is part of the
earth, absorbed into its motion. Her years are "earthly"
years; her course is "earth's diurnal course." We are time's
prisoners, the poem says, and we die in prison.

3

The Nature and Status of the Mind

Although Wordsworth sometimes seemed to speak slightingly of science (see *Excursion,* 4:941–94), he certainly accepted the Newtonian view of a universe whose motion is predictable and regular. The experiences of disordered time which he records in the poems I have examined in the previous chapter he seems to recognize as arising from defects or qualities in human consciousness, rather than from oddities in the great continuum itself. The bewilderment is not in the chimes, but in the sensibility of the anxious and wishful listener. For the mind is not merely a thing that thinks, but a thing that thinks about itself. In the fragment of *The Recluse* which he published as part of his Preface to *The Excursion* (1814), Wordsworth speaks of the fear and awe which "fall upon us often when we look / Into our Minds, into the Mind of Man" (ll. 38–40). Although he never in his work formally debated the question of whether or not the mind constitutes a ghost in the machine, there is evidence in it that, for Wordsworth, one of the most important subjects of the mind's self-reflecting curiosity is its own nature. Does the mind share the vulnerability of the nervous and physiological machinery which it appears to be using? Lord Byron recommends that we wait for the time when we shall all *know,* or at least lie still. For Wordsworth the pattern of belief was probably similar to that of Bishop Blougram's chess board, chequered equally by faith and doubt.[1] It is this uncertainty, perhaps, or rather a series of opposed alternating certainties, that muddles the Hambleton Hills sonnets. At this stage of my inquiry, then, I shall need to examine as best I can Wordsworth's ideas about the nature of the mind. I shall not, however, spend too much time trying to fish out an epistemology. Although very few people read Wordsworth in order to find or to ratify a system of beliefs, many students and commentators still feel that they ought to be able at least to identify such a system. It is safer for such readers to think in terms of notions derived from philosophy or intuitions reinforced by philosophical thinking, held in the back of the mind and reaching the page more in the form of controlling principles of imagery and language than of propositions for belief. My main purpose now is to establish what Wordsworth's assumptions about the nature of the mind were, in order to describe properly his vision of the mind's interaction with the time-world "out there" and analyze more fully the vividness of that encounter.

The best place to begin is with "Lines Composed above Tintern Abbey"; it is also the most hazardous, for it is in this poem that readers may be most tempted to play hunt-the-system. Alan Grob, for example, speaks of "the depth of Wordsworth's commitment to the empirical" during the period when "Tintern Abbey" was written, citing in evidence metaphors in which the mind is represented, not as an organism with potentiality for growth, but "as something moulded from without, an art form or an artefact, or in even more commonplace terms, a piece of masonry put together from what Coleridge contemptuously calls the 'bricks and mortar' of sensation."[2] The particular aspect of empiricism which Grob wishes to emphasize is associationism, and there is support for this emphasis in "Tintern Abbey," where Wordsworth asserts that nature and her beauteous forms not merely inform the mind, but "impress" it (and the sense of the word seems to be "stamp a pattern on") with quietness and beauty and feed it with lofty thoughts (ll. 5–7, 125–28). The forms of nature as perceived by human senses are thus seen as the sources of moral sensibility (ll. 107–11).

There is also a good deal of corroboration for Grob's view of Wordsworth's associationism in book 1 of *The Prelude,* where the emphasis on repetition and reinforcement not merely looks back to David Hartley, but forward to B. F. Skinner and the behaviorist school of psychology. Indeed, lines 599–612 read like a versified account of the techniques of behavior modification therapy.

> The scenes . . .
> Remained in their substantial lineaments
> Depicted on the brain, and to the eye
> Were visible, a daily sight; and thus
> By the impressive discipline of fear,
> By pleasure and repeated happiness,
> So frequently repeated, and by force
> Of obscure feelings representative
> Of things forgotten, these same scenes so bright,
> So beautiful, so majestic in themselves,
> Though yet the day was distant, did become
> Habitually dear, and all their forms
> And changeful colours by invisible links
> Were fastened to the affections.

There are equally "doctrinal" passages in shorter poems, as in lines 17–24 of "Expostulation and Reply."

> 'The eye—it cannot choose but see;
> We cannot bid the ear be still;
> Our bodies feel, where'er they be,
> Against or with our will.

'Nor less I deem that there are Powers
Which of themselves our minds impress;
That we can feed this mind of ours
In a wise passiveness.'

There is no doubt that Wordsworth, during the period
1797–1805 that Grob is concerned with, gave a general assent
to associationist principles, most probably finding in them a
means whereby human nature might be born again in spite of
the disappointment of the French Revolution. But in speaking of the depth of Wordsworth's commitment to associationism, Grob overstates his case, for there are easily
identifiable elements in the poetry which imply more active
and independent properties of the mind. Grob tries to accommodate these difficulties in a passage which reads like a
dismissive concession.

> To speak of mind as essentially passive in its relation to the
> principal source of its experience does not mean, however,
> that it is altogether passive, that in every instance our per-
> ceived experience is received by us completely independent of
> our own acts and choices. Any empirical theory must, to
> some extent, make allowances for a limited number of inter-
> nal controls over what materials finally present themselves to
> consciousness and even over the forms these materials will
> take. That is, there is an indisputable element of willed activ-
> ity in such mental processes as choosing to attend to the ex-
> ternal world, or, oftentimes, even in selecting an object from
> that world on which to concentrate. Recollection, too, seems
> in some cases to involve processes of selection inexplicable
> solely on the basis of associationism's automatic shuffling of
> stored images.[3]

This is much like the tired joke about being a little bit preg-
nant. What he wants to say is that the mind can choose what
to attend to, but it cannot choose what to be influenced by or
how it will be influenced. But once we have allowed the
mind the initiative of choice, where and how do we recognize

the limits of choice? Some of Grob's phrases represent a desperate plugging of the dykes: the theory "must, *to some extent,* make allowances for *a limited number* of internal controls" (my italics). Clearly it must, to meet the test of living. Meanwhile, an innate principle has slipped in.

I do not suppose that Grob intended to defend the theory of associationism itself. What involves him in this awkward business is his judgment that Wordsworth was deeply committed to empiricism and that "Tintern Abbey" and other poems of the period reveal an associationism more radical than Hartley's. The difficulty is that precisely the kind of concession Grob makes is implicit in Wordsworth's poetry. "Expostulation and Reply" illustrates the matter very clearly. The last four stanzas, though ostensibly merely a reply to the expostulation, tacitly assume that the good things which are supposed to happen of necessity are not in fact happening to Matthew, though his environment is and has long been the same as Wordsworth's. If one says that this failure occurs because Matthew has not adopted the "wise passiveness" that Wordsworth recommends, then one admits that such a posture is necessary and can be chosen.

The companion poem, "The Tables Turned," more explicitly recommends an act of submission.

> Enough of Science and of Art;
> Close up those barren leaves;
> Come forth, and bring with you a heart
> That watches and receives.
>
> (Ll. 29–32)

These lines not only concede that it is possible to refuse to submit, but that Matthew *is* refusing. And if it is objected that Matthew is too old for the process to work (it belongs to the first, "thoughtless" stage of life), then it may be pointed out that the Dorothy Wordsworth addressed in "Tintern Abbey" is not—yet William devotes a lengthy passage of exhortations to her. What is urged upon both Matthew and

Dorothy is cooperation with nature, an exposing of the sensibilities to its benevolent influence. Associationism in itself should not postulate the need for such cooperation, for cooperation implies a view of the mind as being capable of choice and independent activity.

I have perhaps just identified the principal difficulty in seeing associationist statements in Wordsworth's poetry, but it is not the only one. The very nature of poetry also constitutes a problem, for poetry necessarily involves judgment, selection, and the reordering of remembered experience. Geoffrey Durrant comments on "Tintern Abbey":

> Only a mind wakened to passionate contemplation could so analyse and order a scene which for most of us would have been merely pretty. What the passage tells us then—what Wordsworth says throughout the poem—is that the mind of man "half creates" what it sees, and that the world "of eye and ear" depends for the revelation of its beauty and order on the activity of the observing mind. . . . Its power of refreshment comes from its reminder of the powers that are latent in all human minds.[4]

There is also the problem of the specially significant moment. In "Tintern Abbey" Wordsworth explicitly evaluates one such: "in this moment there is life and food / For future years" (ll. 64–65). David Perkins has said that no purely sensationalist theory of mind "can account for the decisive importance of a few particular moments. One requires, instead, a psychology showing that the mind unconsciously determines what will determine it."[5]

Let me now try to make a more limited and possibly more defensible claim than Grob does. Is it not safe to say: associationism was attractive to Wordsworth because it seemed to give a basis for the value he attached to his relationship with nature at this time; it offered the possibility of an optimistic view of people and things which he desperately needed; and, consequently, it helped to form the images and influenced the diction in which he expresses the relationship and the optimism? Can one in fact say simply that it was a source of figurative language rather than a creed? Unfortunately, no; not simply that, as lines 121–34 of "Tintern Abbey" reveal.

> this prayer I make,
> Knowing that Nature never did betray
> The heart that loved her; 'tis her privilege,
> Through all the years of this our life, to lead
> From joy to joy: for she can so inform
> The mind that is within us, so impress
> With quietness and beauty, and so feed
> With lofty thoughts, that neither evil tongues,
> Rash judgments, nor the sneers of selfish men,
> Nor greetings where no kindness is, nor all
> The dreary intercourse of daily life,
> Shall e'er prevail against us, or disturb
> Our cheerful faith, that all which we behold
> Is full of blessings.

The word "prayer" points the implication of the whole passage and sets off echoes. The "neither... nor" clauses of lines 128–31 remind one of Romans 8:38–39, where Saint Paul proclaims that nothing can separate Christians from the love of God. Lines 132–33 recall Matthew 16:18, where Christ promises that the gates of hell shall not prevail against the church, and Luke 22:31–32, where Peter is assured that his faith will not fail. I should also note a similar echo in *The Prelude*, 2:443–44: "a more than Roman confidence, a faith / That fails not." There is, of course, more directly religious language in "Tintern Abbey." Wordsworth is a "worshipper" with a deep zeal of "holy love."

These biblical echoes do not constitute an attempt to baptize the "infidel" notions of Locke and Hartley. It may be that Wordsworth, perhaps unconsciously, is merely borrowing from the New Testament a confident tone which he cannot generate for his own ideas. Or the lines may constitute a serious and not irreverent parody of the biblical passages, the purpose of which is to suggest that the group of ideas assembled in the poem makes up a religion which gives Wordsworth the stability and optimism Christianity gives to its believers. Have I then found a creed in the poem after all? Again, unfortunately, no. All this blessed assurance has been undermined earlier in the poem. We have heard, for example, "the still, sad music of humanity." How long can one remain under nature's tutelage, in the security of Brecon or Westmorland, while the French Revolution is being prostituted by Robespierre or the Irish are being massacred at Vinegar Hill? What kind of "moral being" can a man develop if he exposes himself only to the delightful "sensations" of natural beauty and not to the knowledge of what man is doing to man? Human beings need the education of events as well as of nature, as Wordsworth concedes by his very mention of the still, sad music. And there is also the notion that final understanding, "seeing into the life of things," depends upon sense being laid asleep; vision is the privilege of the "living soul."

Furthermore, a strangely false note is struck in "this prayer I make / Knowing that Nature never did betray / The heart that loved her." R. J. Onorato has pointed out the oddity of these lines.

> What is troubling here? Is it just that "betray" sounds too heavily, resonates too inopportunely, having its own effect against the simple declarative sense of the sentence? One has difficulty imagining in what sense "betrayal" could be applied to Nature.

But the matter is not really accountable in Onorato's terms, which are that nature is a surrogate for Wordsworth's mother, who may be said to have betrayed him by dying when he was only eight.[6] This is too conjectural and distorts the meaning of "betray." Possibly Wordsworth is comparing nature favorably with living men who do betray—leaders of the French Revolution, for example. But the curiously gratuitous assertiveness of "betray" also may be accounted for by Wordsworth's knowledge that the fundamental assumptions of the poem are all vulnerable to the assaults of common sense. How much easier it is to believe in the hippogriff than in the proposition that "all which we behold / Is full of blessings."

I am now in some difficulty, apparently. The greatness of "Tintern Abbey" is indisputable, yet its intellectual basis appears to be nonsense of the sort that reveals itself as such. And if those elements in the poem which appear to imply associationism and the religion of nature constitute neither a statement of belief nor merely a species of figurative expression, what do they constitute? Something similar in nature, perhaps, to the opening lines of Ben Jonson's *Volpone*.

> Good morning to the day, and next, my gold!
> Open the shrine, that I may see my saint!

That there is no formulated creed at the back of these words is obvious; that they are not merely figurative is perhaps a little less so. But the normal work of metaphor is overwhelmed by its function as an intensifying agent—not the comparison but the fervor is the principal effect. We hear too the sardonic voice of the author, for it is Jonson, not Volpone, who is pointing out that the praise exceeds its object. My main concern, however, is to illustrate that metaphorical language can be the voice of rapture rather than a mode of comparison or statement. We need not judge Wordsworth, as we judge Volpone, in order to see that "Tintern Abbey" can be read in a similar way. The false notes then become a necessary part of the tone, a defensive emphasis, almost a parade of the sentiment that is privately known to be excessive and misplaced. Such a reading does not diminish the greatness of the poem; it merely clarifies our notion of its genre. "Tintern Abbey" may be classified as a beautiful and highly sophisticated example of an engaging and vitalizing human phenomenon—the enthusiast's brag. The type is common enough in love poetry, and we even hear the same tone when the poet is apparently at pains to disown bombast: "My mistress' eyes are nothing like the sun . . . / And yet, by heaven . . . " The purpose of Shakespeare's disclaimer is to be itself disclaimed, so that the vaunting may proceed. Wordsworth does something very similar: "If this / Be but a vain belief,—yet Oh! how oft . . . " (ll. 49–50).

There are two cautionary notes one ought to listen to at this point. David Perkins has said: "It may well be that in order to write well a poet must deeply feel the emotion he expresses as he creates the poem, though he need not feel it ever before or after." And E. D. Hirsch has pointed out that the word "enthusiasm" "does imply an optimistic and fervid outlook, but this has little in common with . . . *Schwarmerei*. . . . it is a consistent and disciplined yet highly affirmative way of experiencing things."[7] Rather than talking about Wordsworth's beliefs, then, perhaps it is safer to talk about the assumptions which are associated with his enthusiasm— safer because it is no great matter if different enthusiasms are accompanied by assumptions which are inconsistent with each other. This is surely the case with the early Wordsworth: enthusiasm for nature is accompanied by assumptions about associationism and perfectibility; enthusiasm for the human mind is accompanied by assumptions about imagination and the creativity and judgment of the mind which conflict with associationist principles.

Grob, naturally enough, sees Wordsworth's assumptions about the mind's innate potentialities only as a later development. "We might note that from 1802 onward, figures from biology come to replace constructive metaphors, and their frequent appearance provides a useful index to Wordsworth's growing reliance upon organic explanations of the mind's processes."[8] But both the direct and the implicit inconsistencies in "Tintern Abbey" point surely to the fact that Wordsworth already held an organic view of the mind. Perhaps the least satisfactory aspect of Grob's view of the matter is the language in which he comments on the increasing frequency of those organic metaphors. One wonders, frankly, how much time Wordsworth spent searching for explanations of the mind's processes. Whenever the poet speaks of the mind, he does so with a tone and vigor that has nothing to do with the cool speculative analysis suggested by Grob's terminology.

> Not Chaos, not
> The darkest pit of lowest Erebus,
> Nor aught of blinder vacancy, scooped out
> By help of dreams—can breed such fear and awe
> As fall upon us often when we look
> Into our Minds, into the Mind of Man—
> My haunt, and the main region of my song.
> (Fragment of *The Recluse* in Preface to
> *The Excursion* 1814, ll. 35–41)

> the mind of man becomes
> A thousand times more beautiful than the earth
> On which he dwells . . .
> (*Prelude*, 14:448–50)

Surely these lines reveal the passionate force of Wordsworth's admiration of the mind and his almost trembling reverence as he considers its powers and resources. Such a view of the mind cannot be contained within empirical philosophy, as N. P. Stallknecht, in his discussion of Wordsworth's dissatisfaction with strictly sensationalist theories of knowledge, has so impressively pointed out. For Wordsworth,

> The mind of man, the locus of liberty, is the glory of the world, an awe-inspiring subject for contemplation. Man is worthy of himself only when he realises the dignity and power of which his mind is capable. . . . Unlike the association of ideas or the unconscious forming of habits, this power is not borne in upon the mind by mechanical repetition: it is the fundamental assertion of the mind itself, genuine liberty,

the full exercise of which is at once moral freedom and happiness.[9]

Let us now look at some of the capacities which seem to the poet to make man's mind "the glory of the world." We need not confine ourselves to the great creedal pronouncements and songs of praise such as those already quoted from *The Recluse* and *The Prelude;* Wordsworth's statements about the supremacy of the mind are widely pervasive and often subtly and quietly expressed. Take, for example, what happens in "A narrow girdle of rough stones and crags." When the three idle ramblers meet the emaciated angler, they are moved to compassion and to self-reproach. Grasmere, beautiful as it is, remains a "dead unfeeling lake" (l. 65). And the mind's superiority to nature is also implicit in "She dwelt among the untrodden ways."

> She dwelt among the untrodden ways
>   Beside the springs of Dove,
> A Maid whom there were none to praise
>   And very few to love:
>
> A violet by a mossy stone
>   Half hidden from the eye!
> —Fair as a star, when only one
>   Is shining in the sky.
>
> She lived unknown, and few could know
>   When Lucy ceased to be;
> But she is in her grave, and, oh,
>   The difference to me!

Although "ceased to be" seems to diminish the mind, making it part of the natural order and annihilated at death, this pessimism is in fact necessary in order to identify the particular superiority of the mind which the poem celebrates. The mossy stone (nature) will long outlast the violet (Lucy)—it cannot die because it has never lived—yet it is the violet that delights us, not the stone, and the stone cannot share our delight. And neither the stone nor the single lofty star is disturbed by Lucy's death. Whatever part nature plays in forming our affections, nature has no affections of her own. The difference, says Wordsworth, is a "difference to me!" As Geoffrey Durrant says of this poem: "Wordsworth contemplates the humble place man occupies—or seems to occupy—in the great sweep of space and time, and boldly makes the human mind the measure of it all."[10]

The kinds of sensibility implied in these two examples (the capacity to sense another man's suffering; the knowledge of loss) are not passive or habitual; they are functions of imagination. Stallknecht has made a very good case for Jakob Boehme's influence on Wordsworth's conception of the imagination being ultimately greater than the influence of Locke, Hartley, and Godwin. Wordsworth, he says, shows Behemenist characteristics in his notions of the nature of imagination, the relation of sense to soul, and the origin of mystical vision, as well as in his sense of "*one* life within us and around us," and of the contrast between intuitive wisdom and scientific reason. Imagination seems to be the most important of these. Sensationalist theories of knowledge cannot tolerate the mystical awareness which was so important to Wordsworth, whereas "a philosophy of imagination is not so limited. . . . Imagination aids mystical intuition by achieving a concentration of mental power in one act of attention." Therefore we perceive, as we read the poetry, that "the growth of the poet's mind carries us in its later stages from Godwin to Boehme, from rationalism to a philosophy of imagination and intuitive understanding."[11]

The argument is cogently expressed and has obvious attractions. Nevertheless, looking for a system, Stallknecht brings the light of Boehme to aid his reading of Wordsworth, and sure enough Behemenism bounces back at him from the pages. "There can be little doubt concerning Wordsworth's belief that the imagination is a natural or cosmic or even divine power which unites the finite mind with its environment. This power 'rises' into human consciousness."[12]

Stallknecht may have had in mind the magnificent "abyss" passage from the Snowdon episode in *The Prelude*, 14:63–76. If so, he does not take into account the import of such phrases as "the emblem of a mind," "express / Resemblance," and so forth. There are passages where imagination is seen as a "Power" which sometimes "possesses" the poet, but against these must be set Wordsworth's plain commonsense certainty that there is no imagination in the stone, the star, and the "dead unfeeling lake." Though it may be a reflection of the first great creative fiat, human imagination is native to the human mind.

Geoffrey Hartman supplies a corrective to Stallknecht's view. He sees Wordsworth as discovering, suddenly and with considerable shock, that imagination is a singularly human power and not a natural force. The occasion was the Long Vacation in 1790, when the poet crossed the Alps with his friend Jones. Inquiring the way from an Alpine peasant, the travellers are oppressed by disappointment.

> Loth to believe what we so grieved to hear,
> For still we had hopes that pointed to the clouds,
> We questioned him again, and yet again;
> But every word that from the peasant's lips
> Came in reply, translated by our feelings,
> Ended in this,—*that we had crossed the Alps*.
>   *(Prelude, 6:586–91)*

Nature, to put it simply, had not lived up to expectations. And yet, surprisingly it seems, this account of anticlimax is followed (ll. 592–605) by the most rapturous of Wordsworth's celebrations of the grandeur of the mind of man.

> Imagination—here the Power so called
> Through sad incompetence of human speech,
> That awful Power rose from the mind's abyss
> Like an unfathered vapour that enwraps,
> At once, some lonely traveller. I was lost;
> Halted without an effort to break through;

But to my conscious soul I now can say—
'I recognise thy glory:' in such strength
Of usurpation, when the light of sense
Goes out, but with a flash that has revealed
The invisible world, doth greatness make abode,
There harbours; whether we be young or old,
Our destiny, our being's heart and home,
Is with infinitude, and only there . . .

To understand why this paean should follow the disappointment about the Alps, one must distinguish between the
event itself and how it appeared fourteen years later, when
the poetic account was written. At the time of the event,
Hartman says, Wordsworth's mind "desperately and
unself-knowingly in search of a nature adequate to deep
childhood impressions, finds instead *itself,* and has to acknowledge that nature is no longer its proper subject or
home." By the time of writing, the acknowledgment is
neither grudging nor depressed. The realization has become a
source of joy. "His failure of 1790 taught him gently what
now (1804) literally *blinds* him: the independence of the imagination from nature." Imagination, as Wordsworth says in
lines 592–94, "rose from the *mind's* abyss" (my italics). But
having recognized its autonomy, the mind does not turn
away from nature. Nature may be no longer its proper subject, but it is its proper sphere of activity. Hartman says of the
"rush of verses" with which Wordsworth began *The Prelude*
that they are a kind of self-quotation, "because his subject is
poetry or the mind which has separated from nature and here
celebrates its coming of age by generously returning to it."[13]

Hartman, I think, represents more accurately than
Stallknecht the situation as Wordsworth usually understood
it. For while the mind is both independent of and superior to
nature, its characteristic penchant is for a vigorous and delightful cooperation with nature. In fact, nature and man
seem intended for such creative partnership. Sir Matthew
Hale, whom Stallknecht quotes, speaks of "The admirable

accommodation of Sensible Faculty to the Objects of Sense,
and of those Objects to it, and of both to the wellbeing of
Sensible Nature: The admirable accommodation of the Intel-
lectual Faculty in Man to Intellectual Objects, and of those
Objects to it, and of both to the well-being of the Humane or
Rational Nature."[14] And Wordsworth plainly echoes Hale.

> How exquisitely the individual Mind
>   .   .   .   .   .
> . . . to the external World
> Is fitted:—and how exquisitely, too—
> Theme this but little heard of among men—
> The external World is fitted to the Mind;
> And the creation (by no lower name
> Can it be called) which they with blended might
> Accomplish:—this is our high argument.
>   (Fragment of *The Recluse*, ll. 63, 65–71)

Thus, although the mind is autonomous and imagination
originates solely within the mind, the highest functions of
mind and nature are linked, accomplishing a new creation by
their "blended might." And, we should note, *this* "is our
high argument."

But this new creation is not the only result of the cooperation of mind and nature. The mind itself grows in the
course of its interaction. Nor is this growth the simple aggre-
gation of more and more sensations and their associated feelings, as Grob, and Arthur Beatty before him would imply.[15]
John Danby has said that both Wordsworth and Coleridge
saw the mind as a structured whole, whose growth is self-
ordering, and, "as Wordsworth sees it, growth happens
through the exercise and education of what he sometimes
calls 'emotions', but more frequently 'feelings'—but what we
might prefer to call (equally vaguely) 'experiences'."[16] In
other words, man is not molded by experience, but rather
grows by responding to experience. Examples of this notion
are frequent in Wordsworth's work. In the Snowdon lines,
for example, the poet sees the splendor of the changing ap-

pearances of the earth as the manifestation of a power which
seems to mediate itself to man through nature.

> The power, which all
> Acknowledge when thus moved, which Nature thus
> To bodily sense exhibits, is the express
> Resemblance of that glorious faculty
> That higher minds bear with them as their own.
> This is the very spirit in which they deal
> With the whole compass of the universe:
> They from their native selves can send abroad
> Kindred mutations; for themselves create
> A like existence...
>
> (*Prelude,* 14:86–95)

The mutations sent abroad are "kindred" to those of the
creative power working through nature, and the mind, by its
very reciprocation of that power's activities, both grows and
orders its own growth in such a manner as to create a "like
existence."

We must, of course, no more take this conception of the
mind's interaction with nature as a belief or a philosophy in
what Keats would call the "consecutive" sense than the associationism that Grob and Beatty find. It is a matter of
enthusiasms and assumptions which were energizing
Wordsworth's mind at the time of composition, and these
may not have survived intact the writing of the poem. But if
they did survive, what the poem says (which is what I am
concerned with) is not a theological treatise. Let us take, for
instance, the business of the "higher minds." Wordsworth
says of them: "Such minds are truly from the Deity" (*Prelude,* 14:112). If that is so, what about those of the rest of
humanity? If the minds of ordinary people come from a different source, this is such an untidy implication that a man
setting out a philosophical system would have to devote a
separate chapter to it, or a subsection, or at least a par-
enthesis. Wordsworth himself usually claims a more modest
status for even his most important and apparently assured

statements. The impressively confident ring of the faith that
"Our destiny, our being's heart and home, / Is with infinitude, and only there" should not obscure the subsequent
admission that it is a faith based on hope, effort, expectation,
and desire. Again, note the contrast in the following passage
between the fervent assurance with which belief is expressed
and the nature of the sources of belief.

> I had inward hopes
> And swellings of the spirit, was rapt and soothed,
> Conversed with promises, had glimmering views
> How life pervades the undecaying mind;
> How the immortal soul with God-like power
> Informs, creates, and thaws the deepest sleep
> That time can lay upon her.
>
> (*Prelude,* 4:162–68)

One must take these statements, to use Matthew Arnold's
terminology, for what in themselves they really are—
feelings, assumptions, hopes, expectations, desires, "glimmering views." As such, they may be more vulnerable and
more resilient than argued conclusions. And it is both these
qualities, their vulnerability and their resilience, which makes
them so powerfully generative of Wordsworth's greatest
poetry.

The mind of man is not only independent of nature, it is
a thousand times more beautiful and of a quality and fabric
more divine (*Prelude,* 14:449–54). It holds converse with men
and angels "spread over time past, present and to come / Age
after age, till time shall be no more" (*Prelude,* 14:110–11); it is
Godlike and immortal (*Prelude,* 4:166); its destiny is with
infinitude (*Prelude,* 6:604–5). These statements seem to represent the content of Wordsworth's "glimmering views." But
having noticed the discrepancy between the confidence with
which the statements are made and the diffidence with which
they are introduced, one should not be surprised to find that
Wordsworth experiences from time to time a strange, far-

sighted dismay. The mind is immortal; nature is not. But the mind's expression of itself must be "incarnated," so to speak, in natural materials. But are these incarnate minds, these souls on earth, "immortal," as they are popularly described?

Wordsworth begins the fifth book of *The Prelude* with a lament that the artifacts of man's mind will not be necessary to his "immortal being" (l. 23)—that is, to his life in heaven. He goes on to confess a fear that some worldwide natural disaster might destroy all records of human intellectual achievement. Human life itself, he says, might survive such a disaster,

> But all the meditations of mankind,
> Yea, all the adamantine holds of truth
> By reason built, or passion, which itself
> Is highest reason in a soul sublime;
> The consecrated works of Bard and Sage,
> Sensuous or intellectual, wrought by men,
> Twin labourers and heirs of the same hopes;
> Where would they be? Oh! why hath not the Mind
> Some element to stamp her image on
> In nature somewhat nearer to her own?
>
> (*Prelude*, 5:38–47)

To Wordsworth's "studious friend," this fear must indeed have seemed "going far to seek disquietude" (*Prelude*, 5:53), though to modern man the kind of catastrophe envisaged seems a less remote possibility. But the nature of the disquietude needs to be identified. It is the "garments" of the mind that Wordsworth fears for; ultimately the mind itself is safe. In its final bliss it will not be deprived of the kind of beauty that art offers to living man or of the intellectual joy that philosophy and mathematics offer. But the "garments" will not be needed—thought, poetry, and music will need no grammar and no vibrations. The fair youth beneath the trees will pipe to the spirit ditties of no tone. Words and music are necessary in a world of time and memory, where we must remember the subject while we listen to the predicate and where delight is felt not only in tones but in their sequence. Where all is apprehended fully and simply, there is no call for paper, ink, lips, and breath. But the mind, while not doubting the reality of its ultimate knowledge, clasps its human learning: not Socrates' thoughts only, but his arguments; not Shakespeare's vision, but his poetry; not music, but the strains of music. These latter things we must lose, and these we clutch in panic and would cache away.

It is dread of such loss that shapes Wordsworth's famous dream of the crazed Arab, hurrying across the desert to secure the products of man's mind from destruction by "deluge, now at hand"(*Prelude*, 5:57–140). The sleep in which this dream is experienced is a very light one—a mere doze or catnap in the midday heat of summer. There is very little of the "processing" of the material ingredients which modern dream analysis would expect at deeper levels of unconsciousness. The sea remains the sea, the cave becomes a shell, and the book also becomes a shell that is accepted as a book. In fact, the mental activity is not what we might suppose to be the usual dreaming process—memories of waking life being worked over and transmuted during sleep. The sensuous background of the dream seems to be the real world around the poet, perceived through the lightest veil of sleep and absorbed instantly into the dream. The verse is sonorous with the moan of the sea and the beat of the breakers, reverberating and humming round the cave where Wordsworth drowses.

> 'This,' said he,
> 'Is something of more worth;' and at the word
> Stretched forth the shell, so beautiful in shape,
> In colour so resplendant, with command
> That I should hold it to my ear. I did so,
> And heard that instant in an unknown tongue,
> Which yet I understood, articulate sounds,
> A loud prophetic blast of harmony;
> An Ode, in passion uttered, which foretold
> Destruction to the children of the earth

By deluge, now at hand. No sooner ceased
The song, than the Arab with calm look declared
That all would come to pass of which the voice
Had given forewarning...

(Ll. 88–101)

It is the man who has not been properly asleep who hears buzzing noises in his ears. Those varied *o* and *u* sounds, sometimes combined with the nasal consonants in which the lines abound, and the rhythmic emphasis on "sounds," "loud," "Ode," and "foretold," suggest the murmuring and booming of the sea, distanced by sleep and yet made resonant by the acoustic cave. Yet these effects are not obtrusive; the words chosen are reasonable ones for the narrative purpose. But the sounds are there, inescapably accompanying the events; they are dream noises from the wilderness.

The visual imagery carries the same suggestion of the blending of dream and reality. In a light sleep the eyes may blink open for a second or two, half-seeing the waking world. Hence the sandy wilderness, black and void, is recreated from the sandy beach seen in a glimpse from within the dark cave. The glittering light of the waters of the deep may be produced by a similar half-wakeful flickering of the eyelids, revealing sunlight on a worldly sea. Even the Arab and his dromedary may be the shadows of a passerby—a horseman, perhaps, pausing to make sure that the man in the cave is merely sleeping. And if the reader remembers that this incident may have taken place on the North Lancashire coast, where hundreds of square miles of sand are regularly covered by the tide roaring over Morecambe Bay (often, in fact, as Wordsworth must have known, overwhelming travellers on the treacherous "way of the sands"), the whole basis of the dream becomes more dramatically immediate.

It is also a feature of the half-wakeful dream that we are aware of the peculiarity of dream happenings. A logical part of us remains alert, in a state of suspended protest at what it sees the imagination doing, and afterwards confesses the irrational nature of what was accepted during the dream. Hence the stone and the shell are both agreed to be books, and it is an Iberian Arab who carries them.

> Lance in rest,
> He rode, I keeping pace with him; and now
> He, to my fancy, had become the knight
> Whose tale Cervantes tells; yet not the knight,
> But was an Arab of the desert too;
> Of these was neither, and was both at once.
>
> (Ll. 120–25)

It is worth dwelling on the lightness of the sleep, for it is of some importance that the correspondences between dream and reality are so direct and easy. The more obvious and concrete of these I have dealt with; the rest need to be noted. The Arab rider is a figure created by the memory of Don Quixote and the sands glimpsed from the mouth of the cave. This is why he is a composite figure. The sandy wilderness suggested an Arab and the book suggested Cervantes's hero. But by the same token, the dreamer also becomes a composite figure—partly Wordsworth, partly Sancho Panza, he is skeptical, seeing the stone as a stone and the shell as a shell, yet caught by the logic of the crazed enthusiasm and determined to "cleave unto this man." The Arab's mission itself is the dream version of Wordsworth's going far to seek disquietude: the fear which prompts the mission will seem grotesque in the light of common day, yet may seem both reasonable and real in certain states of mind. Even Wordsworth's studious friend, when, pressed, admits to "kindred hauntings."

The two themes symbolized by the shell and the stone are those that last occupied Wordsworth's waking consciousness, "poetry and geometric truth." The stone represents solid geometry, its contours, hardness, and tangibility suggesting the logic and verifiable reasoning of mathematics. The shell is doubly symbolic of poetry: its bright, dazzling exterior represents imagery and fine phrases, while its sea murmurs carry a message representing the burden of the world's great literature and drama—the vulnerability of man and his works and the urge to fight against oblivion. It also represents the Book of Revelation, prophesying the passing away of the old heaven and the old earth. But the shell is also a transmutation of the cave filled with the sea's reverberations, and, as a symbol of literature, of the book Wordsworth had been reading.

It is also a matter of some importance that Wordsworth does not ascribe equal importance to stone and shell, and neither does the dream Arab. The shell is "something of more worth" than Euclid's *Elements;* the stone represents a reason undisturbed by space and time, but the shell is a god—yea, many gods. There is also an interior parallel to be noticed here. The Arab-Quixote and the Wordsworth-Sancho Panza figures possibly represent, respectively, the shell and the stone. For the Arab-Quixote's mission enacts the prophetic message of the shell, while Wordsworth-Sancho Panza, though caught up in the enchantment of the mission and the message, sees the objects as they really are. He sees the dual nature of the mounted figure and asks sober questions which the inspired rider can hardly pause to answer. But of course the Arab-Quixote figure is really Wordsworth-Arab-Quixote: his valuation of the shell is Wordsworth's valuation; his fear is Wordsworth's fear. Rider and follower, like shell and stone, represent aspects of Wordsworth's mind.

The machinery of the paired images in the dream is a way of dramatizing the division in Wordsworth's thinking I have already glanced at. But there is yet another correspondence to be examined. The light sleep, with occasional surfacings to consciousness, the flickering eyes glimpsing the tide, and the senses filled with sea noises suggest a particular alertness that will not, on this occasion, consent to slumber. Every time the sleeper's eyes open, it seems, it is the sea they look on. And the whole warning of the dream is of "destruction . . . by deluge now at hand"; the "bed of glittering light" is "the waters of the deep / Gathering upon us"; the distress and fear experienced in the very beginning of the dream "Came creeping over me." There is some reason to suppose that Wordsworth sleeps with one eye open, watching the incoming tide. The fear that is the nervous basis of the dream is a perfectly reasonable one, that of being covered by the rising waters of the ocean as they come creeping over the sands of the beach where the poet is sleeping. Yet the fear is not great enough to drive sleep away (it is, then, probably not the fear of being drowned); he would wake up the moment that the encroaching waters began to chill him. It is perhaps the less dramatic fear of merely getting a soaking or having his clothes and his copy of *Don Quixote* spoiled. This normal fear is changed into something perhaps rich, and certainly strange, by the dream consciousness.

The dream fear reflects the value Wordsworth sets on both principal forms of human culture. The stone and the shell, according to Thomas De Quincey, were meant to "illustrate the eternity, and the independence of all social modes or fashions of existence, conceded to those two hemispheres, as it were, that compose the total world of human power— mathematics on the one hand, poetry on the other."[17] Mathematical thought represents immutable pure reason, the most reliable and clear bond between man and man. But literature, the prophetic voice, is a god with the power to cheer and console the human heart. If the world is to be deluged again, these works of man must be made safe. If I take the matter no further than this, I have demonstrated that Wordsworth's enthusiasm for the human mind is, in the purest sense, a humanist fervor. But I cannot leave it there, because Wordsworth has as usual made his own comment.

> Full often, taking from the world of sleep
> This Arab phantom, which I thus beheld,
> This semi-Quixote, I to him have given
> A substance, fancied him a living man,

A gentle dweller in the desert, crazed
By love and feeling, and internal thought
Protracted among endless solitudes;
Have shaped him wandering upon this quest!
Nor have I pitied him; but rather felt
Reverence was due to a being thus employed;
And thought that, in the blind and awful lair
Of such a madness, reason did lie couched.
Enow there are on earth to take in charge
Their wives, their children, and their virgin loves,
Or whatsoever else the heart holds dear;
Enow to stir for these; yea, will I say,
Contemplating in soberness the approach
Of an event so dire, by signs in earth
Or heaven made manifest, that I could share
That maniac's fond anxiety, and go
Upon like errand. Oftentimes at least
Me hath such strong entrancement overcome,
When I have held a volume in my hand,
Poor earthly casket of immortal verse,
Shakespeare, or Milton, labourers divine!

> (*Prelude*, 5:141–65)

This passage makes it more evident that Wordsworth himself is an element in the composite figure of the semi-Quixote. "A gentle dweller... among endless solitudes," setting store on "love and feeling"—these phrases are very obviously applicable to Wordsworth at Grasmere. Nevertheless, the Bedouin is now a maniac; his obsession is "the blind and awful lair" of madness. But in what does his madness consist? In imagining universal disaster to be at hand? Nowadays this conviction may seem unduly pessimistic, but not mad. Wordsworth, however, does not consider this unreasonable fear to be the nature of the madness either. The threat of disaster is a "worst case analysis" merely. The Arab's madness must lie in his response to that worst case, for the clauses which seem intended to justify his priorities ("Enow there are... to take in charge / Their wives, their children") only partly do so. They also remind us of the more natural and humane priorities which would be adopted by the vast majority of people. Wordsworth knows this very well. The other, skeptical, humane part of him, Sancho Panza, knows that the stone is a stone and the shell is a shell, and the message of the shell is valid insofar as its scale of values is healthier than the Arab's. It foretells "destruction to the children of the earth." There is the nightmare, and there is the measure of the rider's insanity.[18]

But poor Sancho Panza is left behind again. Nearly everybody will be busy trying to save human life, says Wordsworth; surely someone will be justified in trying to save cultural works? Common sense says no. If we ever have to build another ark, it is doubtful if we could justify a ship's library. And Wordsworth perhaps admits this when he describes his "Arab" feelings as "strong entrancement." There is also the point that, for Wordsworth, the mind itself is safe in any case. It is only the "garments" that are vulnerable. Again we should note how the implications of this magnify the mind's importance. The works of Shakespeare and Euclid can be dispensed with, because the mind in its eternal element will apprehend beauty and truth without such aids.

Nevertheless, after a second look at the first 165 lines of book 5, it is not the asserted final confidence that establishes itself in the reader's mind, but the sadness and fear. The misgiving is recurrent. In the first 49 lines it is expressed, in the next 4 lines denied, in the next 100 both expressed and denied, in the last 12 or so denied and by implication expressed again. The final image is forlorn.

> I have held a volume in my hand,
> Poor earthly casket of immortal verse,
> Shakespeare, or Milton, labourers divine!

Here again is the division in Wordsworth's thinking which makes him part of both Quixote and Sancho Panza, and which was earlier manifested in the confidence of his statements of faith and the diffidence with which they were introduced. One must suspect that the misgiving is more real than the reassurance and possibly extends to more than the poet is prepared to admit. Going far to seek disquietude may be a matter of going far to disguise the nature of the disquietude. Why this fret about the "garments," since the untrammeled mind is immortal and will in its bliss enjoy a happiness greater than human expression can ever yield? Why, unless it is precisely this assumption that is being questioned?

I have, in the preceding paragraph, used the word "misgiving" with some care. Words such as "faith" and "doubt" indicate positions in which one may, at least temporarily, rest. It seems to me that Wordsworth was never at rest in this sense, for I derive from his poetry an impression of something paradoxical in the exercise of the powers of the mind. Imagination and memory enable us to perceive and in various ways measure time, and thus to recognize that the flow of time is irreversible, and that therefore time has a direction. Hans Meyerhoff has pointed out that this sense of direction in time has in human experience a positive and a negative aspect. In the first case, time is the medium of creative endeavor and achievement.

> The "good" man is the active man, the successful man, the man who has used his time to good purpose.... Time is the essence. Temporal progression is identified with human progress. And time calls for ceaseless striving, activity and production.

But Meyerhoff points out that the negative aspect has been the most common human response: " 'Vanity, vanity all is vanity' sayeth the Preacher." And the belief in "ransoming time through ceaseless striving and/or through the making of a monument enduring for ever is always balanced by the negative perspective."[19]

Wordsworth was certainly aware of this "negative perspective," and his most poignant symbols of the vanity of striving are a pile of stones and a garden run wild. For the universal snag is not merely that all our striving is terminated by death, but that random disaster may render a lifetime's effort futile before death. The fear in Wordsworth's dream of the Arab is that not merely the work of an individual but the whole achievement of man is vulnerable to disaster. And yet Wordsworth, it seems to me, was as unable to relax in the despair these possibilities might point to as he was unable to rest in assured confidence. For imagination and memory, which enable us to perceive our vulnerability, enable us also to conceive of human nature as being able to endure the worst. Even in his vision of universal catastrophe, Wordsworth still speaks of "presage sure / Of day returning and of life revived" (ll. 36–37). For him, then, the real pain of the human situation lies not merely in the fact that the powers of man's intellect generate despair, but also in the fact that his memory and imagination may generate hope. Let us now examine two great narratives in which Wordsworth records the astonishing capacity of man and woman to endure by desperate hope alone the ruin of years of ceaseless striving.

4

Margaret and Michael

It may be true that Wordsworth never achieved a full belief, free from all misgiving, in the indestructible nature of the human mind. Nevertheless, his enthusiasm for the mind and his conception of its dignity remain undiminished by such misgiving. In fact, the fear of its mortality may sometimes appear to render the mind more worthy of awe than orthodox confidence would do. For Wordsworth's reverence is based not only on the mind's energy and creativeness, but also on its capacity for heroism. This is something we see, not in those privileged spirits whose minds "are truly from the Deity," but in such rustics as the old Cumberland Beggar and, notably, the Leech-gatherer, by whose steadfastness Wordsworth's self-pity is rebuked. Nor is this heroism called forth only by old age; when the mind encounters the world, it encounters catastrophe as well as decay, and it is stubbornly reluctant to submit to either. For although, as Geoffrey Hartman indicates, in much of Wordsworth's work the mind which has separated itself from nature celebrates its coming of age by joyously returning to it in delighted cooperation,[1] there is also in some of his finest work a vision of the human mind battling against circumstance. Whatever "new creation" the mind can achieve by blending its might with that of nature, there remains a world out there, full of vicissitude. And there is a kind of nobility of the human mind which shows itself, not in cooperation with nature and the necessities of age and season, but in forlorn resistance to the force of time. Both Margaret of book 1 of *The Excursion* and Michael wage "a foolish strife," preferring to reality a hope which is no longer reasonable. But the force behind that hope is an admirable thing in human nature, an obstinate tenacity in love. Neither of them sought the losing battle; each was pitched into it by the mere hazard of time.

Philip Wayne has seen the story of Margaret as one of the precursors of "the slow-moving rural novel in the manner of Hardy."[2] The general grounds for the comparison are obvious: the protagonists endure slowly increasing anguish until their deaths, the whole action taking place in a rural environment which is presented as something more than mere locale. But there, I think, the resemblance ends. Wordsworth's people have somewhat more control of their destinies than Hardy's, and the universe in which he places them is more genuinely neutral than ominous Wessex. The story of the life and death of the mayor of Casterbridge seems to provide no basis for any real human evaluation of the doomed puppet, but the Pedlar's story of Margaret calls forth a pity that is augmented and made complex by judgment. It is an uncensorious judgment, based only on the Pedlar's own assumptions about the right relationship of people to place and time; it is not derived from dogma and not connected with the supposedly numerous Christian interpolations in the final 1814 text of the poem. Such judgment, by rendering its object genuinely human, releases genuine pity. We do not have to share what Bernard Blackstone has called Wordsworth's "snug Anglicanism" to acknowledge that it is the

fallible sufferer who draws most heavily on our resources of
common human feelings.³ And the judgment, as I hope to
show later, is subject to a hinted final revision.

Wordsworth's method is perfectly fitted to render the
Pedlar's central notion that people have a moral relationship
to time and season. The narrative line is dislocated, necessitat-
ing repeated flashbacks, the narrator is involved in the story,
and we know his history. There is also a subsidiary narrator,
presumably Wordsworth himself, who comments on the
commentary, so to speak. And the comment itself is, with
few exceptions, rendered through the imagery of process and
decay.

The time allusions are at work before the Pedlar begins
his narrative.

> At length I hailed him, seeing that his hat
> Was moist with water-drops, as if the brim
> Had newly scooped a running stream. He rose,
> And ere our lively greeting into peace
> Had settled, ''Tis,' said I, 'a burning day:
> My lips are parched with thirst, but you, it seems,
> Have somewhere found relief.'
>
> (*Excursion,* 1:444–50)

The Wordsworth in the poem recognized significant
matters in retrospect, and so must the reader. Our attention is
perhaps purposely dissipated then, when the first image of
passing time is given. The Pedlar's hat is moist "as if the brim
had scooped a running stream," and Wordsworth comments
that "it seems" that the Pedlar has "somewhere found relief."
It is another forty lines or so before we are given a clue to the
significance of the moist hat. The Pedlar directs Wordsworth's attention to the source from which he has quenched
his thirst.

> It was a plot
> Of garden ground run wild, its matted weeds
> Marked with the steps of those, whom, as they passed,

The gooseberry trees that shot in long lank slips,
Or currants, hanging from their leafless stems,
In scanty strings, had tempted to o'erleap
The broken wall. I looked around, and there,
Where two tall hedge-rows of thick alder boughs
Joined in a cold damp nook, espied a well
Shrouded with willow-flowers and plumy fern.

(Ll. 453–62)

The function of the time symbols in these lines is similar to that of the first few pages of Conrad's *Nostromo*. The defeated Ribiera slouched over his mule, escaping from the Monterists, remains in the reader's memory as a perpetual irony, commenting from just below the surface of consciousness on the ideals and progress of the regime based on San Tome's "material interests." But Wordsworth's dislocated narrative, considered simply as narrative, is less complex than Conrad's. There is, in *Nostromo,* a bewildering pattern of overlapping time sequences; in book 1 of *The Excursion,* after the first flashback to the days of energy and well-being, the successive images of the garden record a simple, unchecked deterioration. It is necessarily simple. Margaret's agony is precisely this: her "foolish strife" takes the form of a distracting hope which progressively isolates her from her natural neighborhood. The "touch of human hand" withdrawn, the garden slowly grows into wilderness.

The passage just quoted, however, is more than a mere end piece at the beginning. The reader becomes an archaeologist, for there are layers of human evidence in the wild growth: "its matted weeds / Marked with the steps of those," and so on. Again one recognizes that submerged working backwards and forwards that belies the comparatively simple narrative order. The garden of the poem's present is in itself evidence of a comparatively distant past, and while we are seeing it in this way Wordsworth draws our eyes to suggestions of a more recent past which at first may seem an irrelevant intrusion. But there is poignancy in thus complicating the reader's time consciousness. Margaret's past is sufficiently overgrown actually to bear imprints of succeeding pasts. Generations are beginning to tread her down, and we are thus prepared for the Pedlar's comment at line 474: "Even of the good is no memorial left." The mention of the later travellers' need to "o'erleap" the wall and of willow-flowers overgrowing the well serve the same purpose as the image of the Pedlar's moist hat. There is an ominous undertone in "cold damp nook" and a memory of dead Ophelia in "willow-flowers and plumy fern." Together the two suggestions point to a simple macabre pun in "shrouded," a pun in which the function of all the time symbols provided by the imagery of unchecked growth is indicated. The wilderness is a natural pall; the decay of the garden is the prolonged, scarcely perceptible burial of all memory of Margaret.

The aspect of the garden in the poem's present is a document, but both Wordsworth and the reader need the Pedlar to decipher its characters.

> "I see around me here
> Things which you cannot see: we die, my Friend,
> Nor we alone, but that which each man loved
> And prized in his peculiar nook of earth
> Dies with him, or is changed; and very soon
> Even of the good is no memorial left."
>
> (Ll. 469–74)

The Pedlar can read the scene before him as the Vicar in *The Brothers* can read the natural prospect of the neighborhood:

> "we all have here
> A pair of diaries,—one serving, Sir,
> For the whole dale, and one for each fire-side—
> Yours was a stranger's judgment: for historians,
> Commend me to these valleys!"
>
> (Ll. 162–66)

But something can be gleaned from the cottage and garden by alert and thoughtful observation alone, without the special

knowledge available from the involved narrator. Wordsworth is in the poem himself partly to represent the reader.
"If you had seen it," the implication is, "thus much you
could derive for yourself." Hence the importance of certain
passages which are related by Wordsworth rather than the
Pedlar.

> Beside yon spring I stood,
> And eyed its waters till we seemed to feel
> One sadness, they and I. For them a bond
> Of brotherhood is broken: time has been
> When, every day, the touch of human hand
> Dislodged the natural sleep that binds them up
> In mortal stillness; and they ministered
> To human comfort. Stooping down to drink,
> Upon the slimy foot-stone I espied
> The useless fragment of a wooden bowl,
> Green with the moss of years, and subject only
> To the soft handling of the elements:
> There let it lie . . .
>
> (Ll. 484–96)

What unaided observation can deduce is a general theme
in the poem. The visible scene contains implicit human
memorials because of a relationship between people and their
natural environment. The closer the relationship, the clearer
the visual record will initially be, and it will fade more
slowly. Wordsworth represents the relationship of the cotta-
gers to their garden as a kind of kinship, so that for the waters
of the spring as Wordsworth sees them in the poem's present,
"a bond / Of brotherhood is broken"; they used regularly to
be disturbed by "the touch of human hand," and in their turn
they "ministered to human comfort." The object which
Wordsworth spies on the "slimy foot-stone," although in
one sense a natural time symbol (ordinary processes of
weathering and decay are the obvious time measures), is full
of human implications. It is a commonplace beech bowl,
carved probably by Margaret's husband from the wood of a

tree near at hand; it has a commonplace purpose, a daily use, and its decay therefore not only measures lapse of time, but it indicates dereliction, a withdrawal of the human touch. "The soft handling of the elements" is reminiscent of a different kind of handling to which the bowl used to be subject; had this not ceased, the bowl would not be broken and green with moss. Similarly the foot-stone would not have been slimy in the time of Margaret's happiness, nor would the Pedlar have had to scoop water in the brim of his hat.

> Many a passenger
> Hath blessed poor Margaret for her gentle looks,
> When she upheld the cool refreshment drawn
> From that forsaken spring; and no one came
> But he was welcome; no one went away
> But that it seemed she loved him.
>
> (Ll. 502–7)

These lines do more than finally make explicit the significance of the moist hat and the moss-green bowl. We can distinguish functional ambiguities, the purpose of which is again that working backwards and forwards. The adjective "forsaken" in its context is a prolepsis, by which the present of Wordsworth and the Pedlar is confused with the past which their imaginations are recreating—the spring was not forsaken when Margaret habitually drew water from it. The confusion is maintained by ambiguities encouraged by line-end pauses.

> *no one came*
> But he was welcome; *no one went away*
> But that it seemed she loved him.

Ostensibly the time is that of Margaret's happiness, yet, because of the rhythmically enforced pauses, the phrases which bear emphasis introduce a desolate note which intrudes into the happy time. The final effect is not of the past being discovered in Wordsworth's present, but of Margaret's happy

present being invaded by the future in which Wordsworth
and the Pedlar now remember her. It is a sensitively managed
premonition.

The special power of the time images I have so far
noticed rests in the fact that their function as time measures
cannot be separated from their function as symbols of the
relationship between people and nature. Furthermore, such a
relationship seems to imply certain moral matters. The Pedlar suggests continually that Margaret and her husband *ought*
to tend the garden and *ought* to offer refreshment to travellers; as long as they continued to do so they were fulfilling a
natural obligation. This obligation is not simply to a piece of
land or a cottage; it is also an obligation to time and season in
the sense of John 9:4: we must "work while it is yet day."
Thus Margaret's pride arises not merely from her husband's
energy, but from the kind of natural righteousness manifested in his industry.

> She with pride would tell
> That he was often seated at his loom,
> In summer, ere the mower was abroad
> Among the dewy grass,—in early spring,
> Ere the last star had vanished.—They who passed
> At evening, from behind the garden fence
> Might hear his busy spade, which he would ply,
> After his daily work, until the light
> Had failed, and every leaf and flower were lost
> In the dark hedges. So their days were spent
> In peace and comfort.
>
> (Ll. 523–33)

His hard work is measured against both natural and social
time scales: "In summer, ere the mower was abroad"; "in
early spring / Ere the last star had vanished"; and "They who
passed / At evening." Margaret's husband not only works
before others have begun and carries on after others have
stopped, he continues till even nature insists on rest: "until
the light / Had failed." "So," says the Pedlar, meaning prob-

ably both "in this manner" and "because they lived in this
way," "their days were spent / In peace and comfort."

This industrious cooperation with time and place is well
and good so long as time and place remain reasonably benevolent, carrying out, one may say, their side of the bar-
gain. However, the problem of "evil times" remains. In lines
535–64, the Pedlar tells Wordsworth of such times having
befallen the district less than twenty years previously. War
and two bad harvests in succession had reduced many rich
people to poverty, thrown many artisans out of work, and
caused the deaths of many of the poor. Margaret had endured
the common afflictions with cheerful self-discipline, but she
began to experience particular troubles. First her husband
suffered a long and debilitating illness, and by the time he had
recovered, the little money he had set aside against such mis-
fortunes had been spent. Next a second baby was born, adding another call on the couple's scanty resources. The passage
compels us to examine briefly the manner in which
Wordsworth applies epithets of quality to nouns such as
"time," "season," and "hour." Certain phrases, such as
"Two blighting seasons" (l. 537), "The hardships of that
season" (l. 543), and "those calamitous years" (l. 549) seem
almost to imply that some personified abstraction—Time, or
Season, or Year—is being willfully malevolent.

Something similar is suggested in "The Last of the
Flock." The poem gives no reason for the withering away of
the flock. There is certainly no hint of a failing on the
shepherd's side, nor is any material disaster explicitly named.
All we are told, with insistent repetition, is that times were
bad: "a time of need," "A woeful time," "an evil time," and
the refrain of three stanzas, "For me it was a woeful day."
There is, to be sure, an assertion that God visits the affliction
on the shepherd, but we are not told what in the shepherd
God is punishing. Wordsworth seems, both in "The Last of
the Flock" and in the *Excursion* passage, to be simply and
superstitiously attributing to the abstraction "time" a capacity for spite or cruelty. We are ready to smile at such stuff and

point out that it was the weather, or the soil, or the liver
fluke, or agricultural technology, or the government that was
bad, not the time—at which Wordsworth might smile in his
turn, if he were much given to smiling, and suggest that this
was the point he thought he had made.

Wordsworth habitually describes significant time, not
merely by using abstract nouns provided by clock and calendar, but by picking out the special moment as a stage in
continuing change in nature, in the habits and processes of
human life, or in the relationship of natural and human life to
each other—the total state of affairs, in fact, *then*. Thus the
awareness of time that Wordsworth encourages in our minds
is an awareness of perceptibly concrete matters and of human
responses to them. Wordsworth is being neither simple-
minded nor superstitious in his handling of time; on the contrary, he is, in a certain obvious sense, being scientific. We
may define time as a measure of the rate of change in nature,
but our consciousness of time is complicated by our human
responses to the changes themselves. Thus, in line 537, "Two
blighting seasons" is a superb pun, suggesting both disease in
crops and shriveled hopes. As in "The Last of the Flock,"
there is a suggestion that the physical blight was sent by God,
but there is no attempt to justify God's action. The opportu-
nity to regard it as punishment for the human wickedness of
war is ostentatiously not taken—and wisely so, for Margaret
and Robert had made war on no one.

This lack of justification is clearly not an oversight on
Wordsworth's part; his purpose is not Milton's. The importance of the disaster lies not in the disaster itself, but in the
human response to it, which may be true also of lines 2–4 of
"The Last of the Flock." Perhaps there is disapproval as well
as horror and pity in "I have not often seen / A healthy man,
a man full grown, / Weep in the public roads, alone." And
one can hardly doubt the approbation expressed in the Pedlar's "gladly reconciled / To numerous self-denials, Margaret
/ Went struggling on through those calamitous years / With
cheerful hope" (ll. 547–50). As long as Margaret maintains

this active courage, she continues to live in the real world. Margaret and her husband's failure is not one of initial response, but of lack of perseverance in that response. It is the man's courage that ebbs first. His running away is merely the final acknowledgment of capitulation, for the evidence of defeat is there long before his flight.

> At the door he stood,
> And whistled many a snatch of merry tunes
> That had no mirth in them; or with his knife
> Carved uncouth figures on the heads of sticks—
> Then, not less idly, sought, through every nook
> In house or garden, any casual work
> Of use or ornament; and with a strange,
> Amusing, yet uneasy, novelty,
> He mingled, where he might, the various tasks
> Of summer, autumn, winter, and of spring.
> But this endured not.
>
> (Ll. 568–78)

The weaver's merriment is artificial, reflecting the artificial nature of his occupation. The jobs he does about the cottage and garden are "uneasy novelties," untimely and finally unsatisfying. The specious industry and its accompanying forced gaiety are necessarily brief; the man's energy, isolated from the natural cycle, inevitably decays, and his increasing lethargy is reflected in the pace of the verse.

> day by day he drooped,
> And he would leave his work—and to the town
> Would turn without an errand his slack steps;
> Or wander here and there among the fields.
>
> (Ll. 581–84)

The suspended syntax and the final rhythmic drag of long vowels in lines 581–82 underline the point. He is without the purpose which kinship with time and place once gave him (his wandering "here and there among the fields," one might note, parallels his mingling the tasks of the seasons), and purposeless activity naturally decelerates. Margaret's courage is more durable. The Pedlar describes a leave-taking which occurred after she had told him of finding the little parcel of money left by her enlisted husband. She has taken over her husband's tasks; but although her mood is one of admirable resolution, there is a premonitory forced note in her cheerfulness: "with a brighter eye she looked around / As if she had been shedding tears of joy" (ll. 688–89); "a voice / That seemed the very sound of happy thoughts" (ll. 695–96). Nevertheless, the relationship with season and natural environment is maintained, and only when this fails will the fatal processes begin.

At this point in the narrative occurs a passage full of Wordsworthian guile. The Pedlar gives a brief summary of his journeyings before he next saw Margaret. The tone is one of swinging blitheness and tough endurance; the stride of the verse is long, rapid, and regular; the marcher seems to be singing or whistling on his way.

> 'I roved o'er many a hill and many a dale,
> With my accustomed load; in heat and cold,
> Through many a wood and many an open ground,
> In sunshine and in shade, in wet and fair,
> Drooping or blithe of heart, as might befal;
> My best companions now the driving winds,
> And now the "trotting brooks" and whispering trees,
> And now the music of my own sad steps,
> With many a short-lived thought that passed between,
> And disappeared.'
>
> (Ll. 697–706).

Wordsworth's purpose seems to be to provide a poetic interval, and to do so with an appropriately muscular cheerfulness. The time lapse between the Pedlar's visits to Margaret is indicated, and the reader experiences a breezy relief from the main burden of the poem. But these lines are doing more: a basis for future judgment is being insinuated. The Pedlar is no stock figure of the whistling rover, untouched by pains and difficulty, as are Cowper's heartless postboy and Stevenson's witless tramp. He is not stoical; he is depressed by rain and cold, cheered by warmth and fair weather. He is also saddened from time to time by his loneliness. But although he feels these emotions, he does not, so to speak, entertain them; his moods of depression in particular do not survive the times and seasons that provoked and in a certain sense sanctioned them. Because he neither forces his good cheer nor indulges his pain or melancholy, but responds to the various promptings of the seasons, he endures.

This resilient attitude represents a familiar Wordsworthian doctrine. The ill that cannot be mended must not be allowed to obsess our consciousness; as far as we can, we must respond to what the poet called in "To My Sister" the "spirit of the season." Wordsworth describes at some length his own attempt to adjust in this way in "Ode on Intimations of Immortality," lines 22–24, and the Pedlar suggests the same notion.

> ''Tis now the hour of deepest noon.
> At this still season of repose and peace,
> This hour when all things which are not at rest
> Are cheerful . . .
> Why should a tear be on an old Man's cheek?'
>
> (Ll. 593–98)

These notions having been implanted, we are promptly told that when the Pedlar next called on Margaret, the season was full of splendid promise.

> 'in the warmth of midsummer, the wheat
> Was yellow; and the soft and bladed grass,
> Springing afresh, had o'er the hay-field spread
> Its tender verdure.'
>
> (Ll. 707–10)

Human energies must surely respond to the seasonal exuberance of "Springing afresh." At this point, the Pedlar is suggesting, Margaret ought to become reconciled to the

present; to continue to live in hope, however admirable her
fidelity and resolution, is to be at odds with reality. But when
the Pedlar reaches the cottage, Margaret is not there. He
waits and observes.

> 'Her cottage, then a cheerful object, wore
> Its customary look,—only, it seemed,
> The honeysuckle, crowding round the porch,
> Hung down in heavier tufts; and that bright weed,
> The yellow stone-crop, suffered to take root
> Along the window's edge, profusely grew
> Blinding the lower panes. I turned aside,
> And strolled into her garden. It appeared
> To lag behind the season, and had lost
> Its pride of neatness. Daisy-flowers and thrift
> Had broken their trim border-lines, and straggled
> O'er paths they used to deck: carnations, once
> Prized for surpassing beauty, and no less
> For the peculiar pains they had required,
> Declined their languid heads, wanting support.
> The cumbrous bind-weed, with its wreaths and bells,
> Had twined about her two small rows of peas,
> And dragged them to the earth.'
>
> (Ll. 713–30)

The way the poetry works in these lines demands very close
attention. Paul Sheats has defined the method: "The initial
shift of attention from Margaret to her cottage ... enables
Wordsworth to describe the invisible and painful decline of
the human being by means of the analogous, visible, and
mediating decline of the object."[4] The lines now indicate the
early stages of natural encroachment. The effect is of blurred
edges, heaviness, and weariness. The garden has "lost its
pride of neatness," and the flowers have "broken their trim
border-lines." To notice that the lines are blurred is to notice
that the lines are there—the past is again being seen through
the present which is trying to shroud it. At this stage one
imagines that a few energetic hours would put things right.

But the whole effect of the passage is to suggest that energy is no longer available. The terms used to describe the abandoned flowers and plants—"declined their languid heads" and "dragged to earth," for example—can so easily be transferred to Margaret that, when the Pedlar finally describes her, he need only say, "Her face was pale and thin—her figure too / Was changed." Margaret and the garden together suffer enervation. Wordsworth will use the method of transferred commentary a little later with much more power.

Meanwhile, the involved narrator is hinting at certain judgments. The carnations' heads droop, "wanting support," and there is enough ambiguity in the participle not merely to remind us of the sentience Wordsworth sometimes attributes to daffodils and periwinkles, but to suggest that there is a hint of reproach in the hung heads. But all the details contribute to a major implication: neglect, however caused or excused, breaks not only the bond of kinship with environment but also with time. The garden appears to "lag behind the season." Man, in his closest relationship with the earth, must take notice of the natural calendar; Margaret's husband has earlier mixed the seasons' various tasks, and the Pedlar regarded this behavior as evidence of the beginnings of withdrawal and isolation.

These thoughts prompt the Pedlar to brisk self-reproach: "Ere this an hour / Was wasted." He returns to the door of the cottage to wait for Margaret, whose truancy is now given emphasis. A passerby tells the Pedlar that Margaret is now in the habit of "rambling far," and the extent of her abandonment of her workaday tasks is sharply apparent when the Pedlar hears the baby crying within the cottage. Apparently Margaret habitually leaves it alone for hours. The Pedlar's judgment here is as near the surface as need be, but more subtle forms of judgment emerge from the description of the entrance to the cottage.

'now I first observed
The corner stones, on either side the porch,

> With dull red stains discoloured, and stuck o'er
> With tufts and hairs of wool, as if the sheep,
> That fed upon the Common, thither came
> Familiarly, and found a couching-place
> Even at her threshold. Deeper shadows fell
> From these tall elms; the cottage-clock struck eight,—
> I turned, and saw her distant a few steps.
> Her face was pale and thin—her figure, too,
> Was changed.'

                                                                    (Ll. 742–52)

Every item here has a purpose in addition to description,
producing the sense of a major dislocation of Margaret's relationship to her environment. The detail "corner stones" has
obvious symbolic importance, and "tufts of hair and wool"
suggest more than untidiness and unmended fences. The
sheep come where, in a more normal relationship between
people and place, they would not come "familiarly." They lie
down and sleep on Margaret's very doorstep. "Deeper shadows" carries the same sort of symbolic double entendre as
"corner stones," and the striking of the clock has the same
reproachful resonance as the adjective "wanting" had earlier.
The most significant attribute of Margaret in this particular
glimpse of her is implied in the epithet "distant." The Pedlar
sees her a few steps away from the cottage, but she is "distant" in a far more serious sense, and her physical truancy
springs from and emphasizes her fatal alienation. The bond of
brotherhood is broken, the touch of human hand withdrawn,
and the garden lags behind the season. The Pedlar offers no
rebuke, but Margaret seems to read a comment in his gaze.

>   "I perceive
> You look at me, and you have cause; to-day
> I have been travelling far; and many days
> About the fields I wander, knowing this
> Only, that what I seek I cannot find;
> And so I waste my time."

                                                                    (Ll. 762–67)

Like Robert, who also wandered about the fields before his desertion, Margaret wastes time knowing it to be waste; her hope can now exist only in fantasy, and fantasy can only be nourished at the cost of a relaxed grip on real life.

> 'In every act
> Pertaining to her house-affairs, appeared
> The careless stillness of a thinking mind
> Self-occupied; to which all outward things
> Are like an idle matter.'
>
> (Ll. 795–99)

It is easy to suppose that aestheticism, drugs, and daydreams are the only forms that fantasy living can take. But the Pedlar is here suggesting a less common, though no less seductive, retreat. Margaret prefers the subtly addictive pain of unjustifiable hope to common reality. Nonetheless, while the form of her dependency may differ, the penalty is the common one. The wages of fantasy living is death.

On the Pedlar's next visit, Margaret's withdrawal from the business of common life has become more evident. The floor of her cottage is damp and untidy, there is no fire in her hearth, and her little store of books is scattered in disorder. Her garden is untilled and overgrown with weeds and grass. Wordsworth points to the ultimate implication of this decay by means of a most poignant ambiguity.

> 'a chain of straw,
> Which had been twined about the slender stem
> Of a young apple-tree, lay at its root;
> The bark was nibbled round by truant sheep.
> —Margaret stood near, her infant in her arms,
> And, noting that my eye was on the tree,
> She said, "I fear it will be dead and gone
> Ere Robert come again."'
>
> (Ll. 839–46)

Both Margaret and her garden are dying and for the same reason: Margaret's dereliction of her duties to time and place

(or, in simple terms, to the real world in which she must
live). Margaret is guilty of truancy, but the reproachful
epithet "truant" is applied to the sheep whose nibbling at the
bark will be fatal for the young tree. When Margaret appears
to be prophesying the death of the tree, she has her baby in
her arms, and, the Pedlar tells us

> 'when,
> In bleak December, I retraced this way,
> She told me that her little babe was dead,
> And she was left alone.'

(Ll. 854–57)

One begins to see that the transference mechanism has
another purpose besides the plain one of emphasizing the
relationship which is now betrayed. Everything that is reproachful of Margaret is by this means distanced and muted.
The judgment is never plainly stated and is rarely an immediate inference; it emerges surreptitiously and gently from
the reader's full consciousness of the whole narrative.

The reader is not entirely unprepared for the baby's
death, even if he has not noticed the transference mechanism
and the ominous placing of the infant as Margaret makes her
prophecy. The babe "Had from its mother caught the trick of
grief." Presumably the baby dies because it is infected with
its mother's despair: "but for her babe / And for her little
orphan boy, she said, / She had no wish to live" (ll. 848–50).
There is enough ambiguity in "but for" to allow the
momentary sense that Margaret speaks for her children, not
merely about them.

Margaret's truancy is a withdrawal from the present and
an attachment to the ghost of the past. The idleness of this
attachment is suggested by yet another transferred epithet.

> 'I saw the idle loom
> Still in its place; his Sunday garments hung
> Upon the self-same nail; his very staff
> Stood undisturbed behind the door.'

(Ll. 851–54)

And the next thing the reader is told is that the baby is dead. If Margaret had directed sufficient energy to the business of present living, she would have dismantled this shrine. As Sheats has said, "The image records the decay of her industry and . . . of the self-preserving energies of her mind."[5]

The dominant feeling towards Margaret expressed by both Wordsworth and the Pedlar is, however, compassion, not disapproval. Although there is a large element of judgment in the Pedlar's account, it is never explicitly voiced. Far more prominent is the sense of fellow-feeling that the judgment makes possible; it is so great at times that the Pedlar is more cast down than the woman to whom his sympathies are rushing.

> 'I had little power
> To give her comfort, and was glad to take
> Such words of hope from her own mouth as served
> To cheer us both.'
>
> (Ll. 683–86)

The same lines indicate that Margaret's response to catastrophe was far from spineless or self-pitying. (She has just told the Pedlar of finding the parcel of money.) She is never completely paralyzed in will; she continues for some time to work busily at her usual tasks, and the decay in cottage and garden is slow, though cumulative. Even at the worst extreme, after the baby's death, when her hope is pathetically forlorn, the stuff of daydreams merely, she is capable of some kind of action. She employs herself in spinning hemp—an occupation bringing little reward but requiring some determined energy and patience. And this last task to occupy her energies also leaves its memorial.

> 'You see that path,
> Now faint,—the grass has crept o'er its grey line;
> There, to and fro, she paced through many a day,
> Of the warm summer, from a belt of hemp
> That girt her waist, spinning the long-drawn thread
> With backward steps.'
>
> (Ll. 882–87)

Though even here there is perhaps a submerged comment in
the last few words.

I should also note the due apportionment of blame
suggested in the Pedlar's conclusion of his tale.

> 'Meanwhile her poor Hut
> Sank to decay; for he was gone, whose hand,
> At the first nipping of October frost,
> Closed up each chink, and with fresh bands of straw
> Chequered the green-grown thatch.'

(Ll. 900–904)

Although morally and psychologically truant, Margaret will
not physically desert the home she can no longer maintain.
The hope that binds her to it may be a matter of fantasy, but
it is a fantasy prompted by the stubbornness of human affec-
tion.

> 'still that length of road,
> And this rude bench, one torturing hope endeared,
> Fast rooted at her heart.'

(Ll. 912–14)

The substance of her torturing hope is her husband's return.
Margaret's breach of faith with the seasons is occasioned by
the increasingly exclusive claims of her fidelity to the memory of the man who abandoned her, and his dereliction is
represented as directly hastening her death. The chinks are
not closed up, the thatch is not mended, and on a stormy day
Margaret shivers by her fireside.

The Pedlar adds a devout postscript, telling Wordsworth not to grieve for one who maintained her religious
faith and had often experienced the deepest kind of spiritual consolation. The Pedlar's ethical substance has been
molded by his church, and no doubt Wordsworth could
argue that such a man might naturally express such a reflection. Nevertheless, the effect of the Pedlar's words is to bring
a comfort which sounds spurious because it appears to come

from outside the poem; consequently the lines merely sound thinly doctrinaire. However, the invaluable auxiliary narrator balances the Pedlar's obtrusive piety, and the poem has a more fitting end in Wordsworth's last look at the garden, where he still perceives Margaret's energy and devotion.

> Then towards the cottage I returned; and traced
> Fondly, though with an interest more mild,
> That secret spirit of humanity
> Which, 'mid the calm oblivious tendencies
> Of nature, 'mid her plants, and weeds, and flowers,
> And silent overgrowings, still survived.
>
> (Ll. 925–30)

In these lines, the Pedlar's judgment receives that final modification that I spoke of earlier. If the abandoned garden records Margaret's defeat (and the Pedlar has shown in detail, stage by stage, that it does), it also records how long she endured.

Wordsworth was writing the substance of book 1 of *The Excursion* between 1795 and 1798. Towards the end of this period he may well have been pondering the subject of "Michael," for the old shepherd's story is sufficiently like Margaret's to suggest a deliberate return to the earlier theme. Both poems record lives of thrift and industry blighted by economic accident, desertions by someone deeply loved, and the loss of energy and purpose as a result of those desertions. The family in the Evening Star are quite as energetic and provident as Margaret and Robert, and their only rest is at mealtime.

> Yet when the meal
> Was ended, Luke (for so the Son was named)
> And his old Father both betook themselves
> To such convenient work as might employ
> Their hands by the fire-side...
>
> . . . . .
>
> while far into the night

The Housewife plied her own peculiar work,
Making the cottage through the silent hours
Murmur as with the sound of summer flies.

(Ll. 102–6, 125–28)

Again like Margaret and Robert, they at first respond resil-
iently to calamity. Although it is true that when Michael
hears of the new burden laid upon him, the news takes "more
hope out of his life than he supposed / That any old man ever
could have lost" (ll. 219–20), nevertheless he has soon
"armed himself with strength" and conceived the scheme of
sending Luke to their prosperous kinsman, hoping that by his
industry he will recover their fortunes. Isabel is soon thinking
of the encouraging history of Richard Bateman, the parish
boy who at his death left estates and money to the poor. Her
face brightens at the thought, and Michael is cheered: " 'this
scheme / These two days has been meat and drink to me' "
(ll. 274–75). After Luke has been sent away,

The Shepherd went about his daily work
With confident and cheerful thoughts; and now
Sometimes when he could find a leisure hour
He to that valley took his way, and there
Wrought at the Sheep-fold.

(Ll. 438–42)

Even after Luke, disgraced and ashamed, exiles himself to
foreign lands, Michael still goes through the motions. But
the difference in his spirit is felt in the poetry.

And to that hollow dell from time to time
Did he repair, to build the Fold of which
His flock had need.

(Ll. 460–62)

Soon the journeys to the fold become merely a sorrowful
habit; the nerve for action is dead.

> many and many a day he thither went,
> And never lifted up a single stone.
>
> (Ll. 465–68)

The similarities between "Michael" and book 1 of *The Excursion* can thus be summed up briefly and tidily; the differences show themselves in a more general examination of "Michael."

One of the most noticeable peculiarities of the poem is an obtrusive preciseness about time. The reader can make a reasonably accurate chart of Michael's life. Beginning from his assurance "'At eighty four I still am strong and hale'" (ll. 389–90), we can gather that he was set to work in the fields before he was fourteen—"'I have been toiling more than seventy years'" (l. 228)—and that both his parents were dead before he was twenty-four. Michael says:

> 'when
> At length their time was come, they were not loth
> To give their bodies to the family mould.
>
> . . . . .
>
> But 'tis a long time to look back, my Son,
> And see so little gain from three score years.'
>
> (Ll. 368–73)

The last line surely refers to the length of time for which the farm has been his, and therefore it seems to have taken him sixteen years to clear the mortgage on the major part of the land: "'Till I was forty years of age, not more / Than half of my inheritance was mine'" (ll. 375–76). We do not know when he married Isabel, but since when Michael tells us he is eighty-four, Wordsworth tells us that Luke was seventeen (l. 123), we know that Michael was sixty-seven when his son was born. Isabel was perhaps fortunate to conceive, for being "full twenty years" (l. 80) younger than her husband, she was forty-seven at her confinement. Michael died at ninety-one, having worked intermittently at building the sheepfold "full seven years" (l. 470). Isabel died at seventy-four (ll. 473–74).

This exactness about time is not only a matter of the general framework. Michael fashions a little shepherd's crook when Luke is five years old; the boy begins daily to accompany his father on his journeying at the age of ten. Michael tells Isabel of his decision to send Luke away two days after he first hears the news of misfortune. Isabel spends five days preparing for Luke's departure before she tries to dissuade him from going, which she does at noon on Sunday. Another week elapses before the welcome letter arrives from their kinsman, and on the following day Luke departs. There is too much of this chronological detail for it to have been accidental or unconscious. Wordsworth evidently intended to produce particular effects, and they must be important. One does not challenge a reader to a half-conscious bout of mental arithmetic without good reason.

In order to identify the effects Wordsworth intended, we must place the time details in relation to certain other details. Because we are used to the banal and tiresome kind of precise detail that Wordsworth allows to his garrulous "supposed narrators" (the sea captain who relates the 'story of "The Thorn," for example), our attention may lapse as we recognize the beginning of such a passage. The first few lines of "Michael" sound as if they should be accompanied by a sketch map.

> If from the public way you turn your steps
> Up the tumultuous brook of Green-head Ghyll,
> You will suppose that with an upright path
> Your feet must struggle.
>
>   (Ll. 1–4)

We need to rouse our attention to look at these details again. In the phrase "You will suppose," Wordsworth is not in fact telling the reader how to get to Easedale, he is merely saying that at the beginning of the ascent the path looks so steep we shall think it is upright. It is not in fact upright, but it is very steep, rough, and difficult, and an enormous contrast to "the public way." A traveller's feet *must* struggle with this path, for there is no easier way. We are climbing to a hidden valley, and Wordsworth is insisting from the outset on its isolation and inaccessibility.

>   they
> Who journey thither find themselves alone
> With a few sheep, with rocks and stones, and kites
> That overhead are sailing in the sky.
> It is in truth an utter solitude.
>
>   (Ll. 9–13)

The path was a sharp contrast to the public way, and the hidden valley is a sharper contrast to Grasmere village. "No habitation can be seen"; there is no village school with its regular hours, no church clock to chime the quarters, no carters, no postboys, no market days and festivals. The time scheme of Easedale and the forest side of Grasmere vale is nature's, "with slow rotation suggesting permanence."

How easily could the persons of a story with this setting take on, in the reader's imagination, the durability of their environment. Michael could become a partly numinous figure like the Leech-gatherer, or an eternal wanderer like the Old Cumberland Beggar. But this must not happen, and hence the need to emphasize his mortality by precise figures. Descriptions such as "Extreme old age" or "The oldest man . . . that ever wore grey hairs" will not do for Michael, because the reader must be aware of his unusual strength and fitness. They are more appropriate for those old men who suffer the expected frailty of old age, and who, because their importance lies in the effect they have on others, and on Wordsworth in particular, can be thought of as spiritually symbolic figures. The reader is not asked to feel with their nerves, but only to feel their effect on his. Michael, on the other hand, is an old man in whose pain the reader becomes involved; therefore, however hale and strong he may be, the number of his years must be plainly stated. All of the figures mentioned in the poem serve this purpose, and the reader may feel that Michael's life should have been enriched with memory and satisfaction rather than with hope even before Luke was conceived.

But Luke was conceived. We now see the more particular purpose of the precise figures given for age. Michael and Luke represent the extremes of youth and age—a situation which always intrigued Wordsworth. (See, for example, "The Fountain," lines 1–4.) Between youth and middle age there may be a barrier of indifference or hostility; youth and old age, surprisingly, seem to have something to say to each other. The growing child commonly finds more sympathy in his grandparents than in his parents. But when the father is old enough to be his only son's great-grandfather, the emotional condition which we may think should accompany old age is disturbed in a manner which, in the nature of things, is likely to be tragic. Wordsworth points this out in a neat ambiguity.

>   to Michael's heart
> This son of his old age was yet more dear—
> Less from instinctive tenderness, the same
> Fond spirit that blindly works in the blood of all—
> Than that a child, more than all other gifts
> That earth can offer to declining man,
> Brings hope with it, and forward-looking thoughts,
> And stirrings of inquietude, when they
> By tendency of nature needs must fail.
>
>   (Ll. 142–50)

There are two meanings compacted in the last clause. First, in old age the capacity for hope and the natural penchant for looking forward must be growing weaker; second, if these qualities are refreshed and invigorated at Michael's time of life, they are likely to be futile, since either they cannot be realized or will not be seen to be realized. If one thinks of a whole human life as having a kind of emotional calendar—as

Keats puts it, "There are four seasons in the mind of man"—
then expectation should not be budding in winter.

The situation is aggravated by the fact that the child of
his old age is Michael's only child. Fatherly emotion is intensified by this late release.

> Exceeding was the love he bare to him,
> His heart and his heart's joy! For often-times
> Old Michael, while he was a babe in arms,
> Had done him female service...
> ... he had rocked
> His cradle, as with a woman's gentle hand.
>
> (Ll. 151–58)

The wreckage of these emotions by the child's going to the
bad would be deeply distressing at any time. In middle life,
however, there may be enough nervous resilience left for the
father to recover from the blow and enough life left for him
to find new satisfactions. But Michael has neither resilience
nor time.

This child of his old age roused not only the paternal but
also the patrimonial instinct. None of the kinsmen mentioned
in the poem seem to have had any thoughts of taking over the
farm; therefore, if Michael and Isabel had had no son, the
fields would naturally have passed into a stranger's hands.
Presumably the thought would have caused them little or no
distress. But as things are, with Luke in his eighteenth year
Michael remarks:

> 'if these fields of ours
> Should pass into a stranger's hand, I think
> That I could not lie quiet in my grave.'
>
> (Ll. 230–32)

Here, very precisely, are those "stirrings of inquietude" (l.
149) that a child brings to "declining man" (l. 147).

At this point I should note that Wordsworth makes very

little comment on Luke's misdeeds. Indeed, he hurries him
out of the poem.

> Luke began
> To slacken in his duty; and, at length,
> He in the dissolute city gave himself
> To evil courses: ignominy and shame
> Fell on him, so that he was driven at last
> To seek a hiding-place beyond the seas.

(Ll. 442–47)

Exit Luke, with hardly a cuff on the ear when he might have
got a birching. We can perhaps understand the leniency if we
understand Wordsworth's purpose. The poem is not basically about filial misbehavior and the pain it inflicts on a
loving father; it is about the disturbance of the whole emotional calendar of a man's life. The spiritual and psychological
seasons are dislocated, and midwinter spring is one of time's
harshest whims.

This disturbance of the seasons of life is the basis of
Michael's tragedy, and the time imagery which marks it out
is necessarily conventional and direct. There are, however,
more subtle and more Wordsworthian time motifs at work in
the poetry. The forms of nature, Wordsworth tells his sister,
"shall be / Our living calendar." Margaret's garden is a visible history, and Wordsworth and the Pedlar peer at it with
the informed perception of archaeologists. In "Michael,"
landscape and natural objects are presented as yet another
kind of commemorative record—a sort of mental photo-
graph album. Wordsworth, we know, cultivated his visual
memory; when he describes the Wye valley, seen again after a
five-year absence, the obtrusiveness of the demonstrative ad-
jectives suggests that the details thus introduced have been
held in his mind and frequently and vividly recalled. They are
merely ratified by the present view: "these steep and lofty
cliffs," "this dark sycamore," "these orchard tufts," "these
hedgerows," and so on. Wordsworth attributes such a visual
memory to Michael, although the shepherd need not culti-

vate it—the incidents and environment of his life are enough
to develop it naturally.

> And grossly that man errs, who should suppose
> That the green valleys, and the streams and rocks,
> Were things indifferent to the Shepherd's thoughts.
> Fields, where with cheerful spirits he had breathed
> The common air; hills, which with vigorous step
> He had so often climbed; which had impressed
> So many incidents upon his mind
> Of hardship, skill or courage, joy or fear;
> Which, like a book, preserved the memory
> Of the dumb animals, whom he had saved,
> Had fed or sheltered, linking to such acts
> The certainty of honourable gain;
> Those fields, those hills—what could they less? had laid
> Strong hold on his affections, were to him
> A pleasurable feeling of blind love,
> The pleasure which there is in life itself.
>
> (Ll. 62–77)

There is no suggestion here of anything which Michael
would rather forget. Every image available to his memory is
satisfying, so no doubt it would have continued had Luke
never been born. But as the child grows up, even more vivid
and persistent images are formed, images that are printed on
the mind, not by a single dramatic incident, but by familiar-
ity and repetition, by observation sharpened with doting
love.

> There, while they two were sitting in the shade,
> With others round them, earnest all and blithe,
> Would Michael exercise his heart with looks
> Of fond correction and reproof bestowed
> Upon the Child, if he disturbed the sheep
> By catching at their legs, or with his shouts
> Scared them . . .
>
> (Ll. 170–76)

Then Michael from a winter coppice cut
With his own hand a sapling, which he hooped
With iron, making it throughout in all
Due requisites a perfect shepherd's staff,
And gave it to the Boy; wherewith equipt
He as a watchman oftentimes was placed
At gate or gap...

       . . . . .

... nought was left undone which staff, or voice,
Or looks, or threatening gestures, could perform.
                                        (Ll. 180–93)

We see in all these cases Luke's postures at each stage of development, dearly familiar to his father and kept lively by that naturally vivid memory. And when Luke is disgraced, the spider love will transubstantiate all.

The loss of Luke's habitual presence is bad enough, of course—Michael is too old to adjust his emotional life to the unexpected deprivation. But he makes some effort to do so. He looks for something that will symbolically link the satisfying memories of the past with the possibility of restored happiness in the future. If he can impress this symbolism on Luke, then the boy will carry with him a memory that will tug him towards home. Thus, though the heap of stones is important in itself, the act of laying the first stone is even more so. The heap of stones represents a present imbued with purpose, the envisaged sheepfold a future to be achieved by perseverance. It is of course true that Michael had intended to build the sheepfold long before this crisis arose, but much more significant is the use he makes of the proposed building as a spiritual link between himself and the absent Luke. As John Garetson Dings points out, the sheepfold now resembles the heap of stones built up by Jacob and Laban (Gen. 31:44–49) and implies a similar prayer: "The Lord watch between me and thee when we are absent one from another."[6]

'When thou return'st, thou in this place wilt see
A work which is not here: a covenant
'Twill be between us.'

(Ll. 413–15)

If the whole enterprise is a covenant between youth and age, its beginning must be experienced as a temporal reference point, a moment of special significance.

'hereafter, Luke,
When thou art gone away, should evil men
Be thy companions, think of me, my Son,
And of this moment.'

(Ll. 404–8)

The attempt fails. Luke gives himself to evil courses and does not heed the memory. Perhaps Wordsworth hints in this poem that the recognition of moments of such significance cannot be willed; they must surprise us, coming when we have at length laid down the burden of thought and effort. Even if we could will such binding experiences for ourselves, almost certainly we cannot impose them on others. If Michael had not identified the moment and the meaning he proposed for it, if he had with apparent carelessness induced Luke to lay the first stone, the symbolic action might have had power in the youth's mind, for the symbol might then have disclosed itself, and Luke's response might have been free. But once an overanxious "meddling intellect" tries to make the matter plain, the moral nudge vitiates the power of the moment.

And so comes the unhappy ending. John Danby finds a positive implication in the poem, seeing Michael's perseverance as something which Michael himself recognizes as part of "the ageless habit of continuing generations... the rich and sombre but never hopeless community of time."[7] But most people assume consciousness to be individual; whatever hope there may be in the situation or in Michael's response to it for the "continuing generations" or "the community of time," there is none for Michael. And since the poem seems to insist so strongly on the centrality of Michael and his pain, most readers will see the ending as desolately unhappy. There is nothing quite like it anywhere else in Wordsworth. "The Affliction of Margaret" is not quite so final; "The Complaint of a Forsaken Indian Woman" is not so gratuitous; the sorrows of Martha Ray are not quite so undeserved. In "Michael," the bleakness is unglamorized and unrelieved. In book 1 of *The Excursion,* the Pedlar offers Wordsworth some conventional religious wisdom, and Wordsworth cheers himself with a more humanistic reflection, tracing in the abandoned garden "that secret spirit of humanity / Which . . . still survives." After the final blow has fallen on Michael, there is no philosophy; all that remains of his labor is the unfinished sheepfold. Except the irrelevant oak tree, all he hoped to preserve is lost.

> the estate
> Was sold, and went into a stranger's hand.
> The Cottage which was named The Evening Star
> Is gone—the ploughshare has been through the ground
> On which it stood.
>
> (Ll. 474–78)

The poet has no balm to apply. Rather, he emphasizes the desolation by banal phrases. "The estate was sold"—the solicitors will deal with outstanding matters. But if there is no comfort, there is also no parade of despair. Wordsworth does not point to the skies and say, "He's a good fellow and 'twill all be well," but neither does he shake his fist at "whatever brute and blackguard made the world." He tells a story from which it seems the only extractable meaning is that this can happen, that time can torture by giving too late, that a virtuous long life can end in seven years of grief.

There is one more thing to be said. Merely to note the restraint with which Wordsworth presents the matter does not sufficiently account for the merit of "Michael" as a poem. There are equally detached accounts of tragedies in coroner's inquest reports. The poem's greatness lies in the marvelous organization of its themes and imagery. To identify this organization, we must look for an informing pattern, one that perhaps reveals itself in a single image where the power and relevance of all other images is made apparent. Such an image may be found, I think, in lines 177–81.

> And when by Heaven's good grace the boy grew up
> A healthy Lad, and carried in his cheek
> Two steady roses that were five years old;
> Then Michael from a winter coppice cut
> With his own hand a sapling.

The boy came to his parents out of season. The roses on his cheeks symbolize both his childhood and Michael's belated fatherhood—emotion blooming in a heart long past its natural summer. Luke is himself the sapling from the winter coppice. And Wordsworth presents this to us as merely one of time's random chances. One could say that the situation was avoidable, and that someone can be blamed for what happened. But the poet does not take this point of view, though it is the sort of position he is often quick to adopt. He reprimands Luke briefly for his misbehavior and hurries back to the real business in hand. For Luke's going to the bad is only the proximate cause of this disaster. It is the child's late advent that gives his father a new sensibility that old age can hardly accommodate, rendering Michael pitifully vulnerable by creating that unseasonable, and therefore fatal, hope. We have always known that time will transfix the flourish set on youth; in "Michael" Wordsworth demonstrates that time also has sophisticated cruelties disguised as late blessings.

The last complexity in the reader's response to both the poems I have just been examining consists in a faint, paradoxical aftereffect. Bleak as their ends have been, their only memorials a derelict garden and a pile of stones, nevertheless, as we look back on the histories of Margaret and Michael, we sense that it is the "secret spirit of humanity" that inspired their foolish strife, and that that is an incorrigible spirit of resistance to nature's "silent overgrowings." However unjustifiable it may be, most people will think it admirable. Wordsworth too, obviously thought it admirable. But he also thought that there was another, more fruitful, way of living with the vicissitudes of time. In place of resistance and stubborn hope for what cannot be, we may adopt a wise passiveness, and in place of ceaseless striving, idleness.

5

Idleness and Deliberate Holiday

In a letter written to William Matthews in
September, 1791, Wordsworth advised him to work hard:
"Hope and Industry are to be your watchwords, and I war-
rant you their influence will secure you the victory." Two
months later he confessed to the same correspondent: "I am
doomed to be an idler thro(ughou)t my whole life. I have
read nothing this age, nor indeed did I ever. Yet with all this I
am tolerably happy."[1] These two sentences might be taken to
indicate that Wordsworth's attitude to hard work was simple
and reprehensible. If we add to these comments the implications of such poems as "Expostulation and Reply," "The
Tables Turned," and "To My Sister" on the one hand, and
book 1 of *The Excursion,* "Michael," and "A narrow girdle of
rough stones and crags" on the other hand, the usual message
of the "spirit of the season" appears to be leisure for poets and
labor for peasants. Wordsworth himself was certainly an
idler. As an undergraduate at Cambridge, he felt he was not
for that hour nor for that place.

> Thus in submissive idleness, my Friend!
> The labouring time of autumn, winter, spring,
> Eight months! rolled pleasingly away . . .
>   (*Prelude*, 3:632–34)

At the same time he sensed the pressures of Cambridge and the anxieties and disappointment of others on his behalf. (Dorothy believed that William could have won a fellowship, had he set himself to it.) But on the whole there is little self-reproach in his references to the matter. What one does sense is a notion that the idleness is not the right sort of idleness—the hours are "pilfered away," the months pass by "remissly." He slips into indolence through sheer aversion to the prescribed kind of activity. Better than this would have been a willed, joyfully defiant idleness.

> My sister! ('tis a wish of mine)
> Now that our morning meal is done,
> Make haste, your morning task resign;
> Come forth and feel the sun.
>
> Edward will come with you;—and, pray,
> Put on with speed your woodland dress;
> And bring no book: for this one day
> We'll give to idleness.
>   ("To My Sister," ll. 9–16)

The idleness to which Wordsworth invites his sister is an active response to the season's regenerative influence. Such idleness is in reality the highest kind of energy, unlike the good-natured lounging of Wordsworth's collegiate life, and is conducive to spiritual growth ("Our minds shall drink at every pore / The spirit of the season," ll. 27–28). And sometimes the nature of the growth is quite specific; the moral gain is identifiable.

I can best make the point by examining one of the finest of Wordsworth's poems on the naming of places. "A narrow girdle of rough stones" deals with how and why Point Rash

Judgment was named. Wordsworth and his two "beloved friends," having spent some part of a calm September morning ambling round Grasmere Lake, see at a distance a man fishing, while from the fields they hear "the busy mirth / Of reapers, men and women, boys and girls" (ll. 40–41). The angler is immediately judged.

> 'Improvident and reckless,' we exclaimed,
> 'The Man must be, who thus can lose a day
> Of the mid harvest, when the labourer's hire
> Is ample, and some little might be stored
> Wherewith to cheer him in the winter time.'
>
> (Ll. 50–54)

Wordsworth has earlier so emphasized the idleness of the three friends that the reader may immediately feel that judgment for judgment is called for. But apparently it is not the friends' own vulnerability that is important; what they must soon penitently acknowledge is that their assumptions about the nature of the angler's occupation were too instant and too easy.

> Too weak to labour in the harvest field,
> The Man was using his best skill to gain
> A pittance from the dead unfeeling lake
> That knew not of his wants.
>
> (Ll. 63–66)

The rash judgment which the poem commemorates appears to be simply this one, plainly stated and plainly shown to be foolish and unjust.

But Wordsworth's better poetry is never as plain as it appears, and, as F. R. Leavis has pointed out in his "Revaluations" essay on Wordsworth that it is most sophisticated in its total effect when on the surface it appears most straightforward.[2] The overt moral lesson which Wordsworth and his friends commit to memory as a place name is the judgment which the three idle ramblers make of themselves.

> I will not say
> What thoughts immediately were ours, nor how
> The happy idleness of that sweet morn,
> With all its lovely images, was changed
> To serious musing and to self-reproach.
>
> (Ll. 66–70)

The phrase "happy idleness" is a hint that their self-reproach included the recognition that they too had been idle—more idle, in fact, than the wasted man whom they had glibly condemned. The first thirty-two lines of the poem, describing their journey round the lake, are worth examining with this recognition in mind, for the passage constitutes a delighted celebration of the joys of idleness. The time reference in lines 7 and 8 ("ere the mist / Had altogether yielded to the sun") is vague, indicating the holiday mood. The verbs contribute to the sense of relaxed, casual enjoyment; the friends, Wordsworth says, "sauntered" (l. 9); "we / Played with our time " (ll. 10–11); "we strolled along" (l. 11); and, "often, trifling with a privilege / Alike indulged to all, we paused" (ll. 26–27). The movement of the verse, stumbling between line endings and caesuras, enacts the interrupted progress of the ramblers.

> And often / trifling with a privilege
> Alike indulged to all, / we paused, / one now,
> And now the other, / to point out, / perchance
> To pluck, / some flower or water-weed / too fair
> Either to be divided from the place
> On which it grew, / or to be left alone
> To its own beauty.
>
> (Ll. 26–32)

Wordsworth is careful to ensure that even this sporadic movement should not become regular. The ear is therefore disappointed of an expected smooth run after "perchance," and a little surprised by the addition of "to its own beauty" after "left alone." The journeying has that sort of arbitrary irregularity that we associate with a consciousness of infinite leisure, of having all the time in the world. And it is precisely because Wordsworth has been at such pains to make the poetry render this that the friends' indignant judgment of the angler is so shocking. A plainer case of the mote and the beam one can hardly imagine, and the point is surely taken by the travellers in their acknowledgment of "happy idleness."

Like Shakespeare's Angelo and Isabella, Wordsworth and his friends do finally judge themselves. But the poem as a whole suggests that their self-condemnation was as wrong as their condemnation of the fisherman. The opening lines make clear that the mood of the ramblers is undoubtedly also "the spirit of the season." There is the same slow, irregular progress, the same unpredictable, irrhythmic stops and starts in the natural objects they see.

> It was our occupation to observe
> Such objects as the waves had tossed ashore,—
> Feather, or leaf, or weed, or withered bough
>
> . . . . .
>
> Not seldom did we stop to watch some tuft
> Of dandelion seed or thistle's beard,
> That skimmed the surface of the dead calm lake,
> Suddenly halting now—a lifeless stand!
> And starting off again with freak as sudden;
> In all its sportive wanderings...
>
> (Ll. 12–22)

We can be sure that the parallels here are not merely aesthetic felicities, for the poem dwells on the "sportive" idleness long enough to suggest a serious purpose. The erratic movements of the dandelion seeds are caused by an "invisible breeze" which is the "moving soul" of the objects skimming the water. The pun on "moving" can hardly be overlooked—the breeze is both moving and the cause of movement. Moreover, it is a Wordsworthian commonplace that breezes are never merely breezes. The "loud dry wind" on the "perilous ridge" is obviously, though vaguely, numinous, and the gentle breeze noted in the opening lines of *The Prelude* is both a visitant and a symbol of the "correspondent breeze" within Wordsworth's mind. It is perhaps not fanciful to suppose that the three ramblers round Grasmere are, like the dandelion seeds, moved by a correspondent invisible breeze, "the spirit of the season."

If I give the opening lines this kind of importance, what am I to make of the rest of the poem? Has Wordsworth irritatingly, but characteristically, disfigured a genuine poetic experience by making a smaller point too plainly? To some extent this is so. The "improvident and reckless" speech has dramatic and ironic justification, but "What need there is to be reserved in speech, / And temper all our thoughts with charity" (ll. 72–73) is indefensibly flat. Nonetheless, even if Wordsworth's overly explicit admonition disfigures the poem, it certainly does not cripple it. The idleness of the ramblers receives its approbation in the experience which arises from it.

The nature of this experience lies in an unexpected recognition.

> Through a thin veil of glittering haze was seen
> Before us, on a point of jutting land,
> The tall and upright figure of a Man.
>
> (Ll. 45–47)

The three friends, like the apostles in the last chapter of Saint John's gospel, do not immediately grasp the significance of the figure before them; when they do, he is described in terms which the disciples might have used of the crucified man whom they saw across the water, standing on the lake shore: "a Man worn down," "gaunt and lean, with sunken cheeks / And wasted limbs" (ll. 57, 59–60). The recognition is shocking and numinous. One is reminded of the specter-thin soldier met at night in *The Prelude,* and, less obviously, of the Leech-gatherer. The man both resembles other Wordsworthian figures and stirs memories of Christ by

Galilee, not merely in points of physical form and setting, but
from the effect of "apt admonishment" that he has on those
who encounter him. The substance of the admonishment is also more complex than the plain statements of the poem. That people
should respond to the spirit of the season is not denied; the
obligation to be guided by the invisible breeze, the "moving
soul" of nature, is not countermanded. But there is a
supplementary moral affirmation: man is more than nature.
Wordsworth and his companions are moved to pity by the
sight of the wasted angler; nature is not. As line 65 emphasizes, the lake is a "dead unfeeling lake." The man, simply by being what he is, puts on the friends the same spiritual
yoke Christ placed on Peter: "Feed my lambs" (John 21:15).
They know, unavoidably, the moral consequences of being
human. Therefore, "The happy idleness of that sweet
morn, / With all its lovely images, was changed"; "Nor did
we fail to see within ourselves" (ll. 68–69, 71). The last
phrase needs no direct object. It is because the happy mood is
changed, because they see within themselves, that the three
ramblers reproach themselves. But they are wrong in their
judgment if (and the poem is not quite clear about this) they
are reproaching themselves for their idleness. For the poem is
quite unambiguous in its demonstration of the notion that
surrender to the spirit of the season led the idlers directly to
the transforming experience. The lesson of that experience is
more important than the wisdom of not speaking out before
knowing all the facts; the vital point taken by the ramblers is
that, although nature may in some sense be a moral guide,
man is what nature is not, a sentient being continually pained
by moral consciousness. Since idleness brought them to this
moment of knowing, it was a good idleness. Their second
rash judgment was of themselves.

The "good" idleness is good because it brings the three
friends to the enlightening experience, but it is also good
because it consists in a therapeutic waste of time, unlike Margaret's waste of time, which merely increased her suffering.

Clock time is forgotten; inner time and nature's time are in harmony. But one may also say that it is good because there is nothing in the poem to suggest that it is bad. In the moral sense, the word "idleness" has nothing to do with the amount of energy being used; it is concerned with duties being neglected, and the seeming idleness of the angler was at first taken to be bad because the sounds from the harvest field suggested something else that he ought to be doing. Nothing in the poem, however, suggests that Wordsworth and his companions were leaving anything undone for the sake of their ramble. Strictly speaking, their idleness is neither good nor bad, for it is not idleness at all.

That a leisured life is not necessarily an idle one is even more true of that of the shepherd in the summertime described in *The Prelude,* 8:196–201.

> at large
> The shepherd strays, a rolling hut his home.
> Thither he comes with spring-time, there abides
> All summer, and at sunrise ye may hear
> His flageolet to liquid notes of love
> Attuned...

Wordsworth is speaking of the best of the shepherd's life, the hours of unlaborious pleasure when Grasmere Vale looks most like Arcady. But even when the rest of the year is taken into account, there is still something enviable in the shepherd's lot. In winter he is called from his hut not just by storms, but by the warning of storms, and he may not wait for warmth before he takes food to his snowbound flock. And in spring,

> when the flock, with warmer weather, climbs
> Higher and higher, him his office leads
> To watch their goings, whatsoever track
> The wanderers choose. For this he quits his home
> At dayspring.
>
> (Ll. 231–35)

Although the rustic atmosphere of the shepherd's time measures tends to conceal their strictness, they have their own
discipline, calling for toughness and perseverance. "Day-
spring" is as commanding as a chiming clock, and the
evaporating dews, as they "Smoke round" the shepherd (ll.
244–45), tell him accurately enough how much is left of the
morning for the performance of its necessary tasks. Nevertheless, nature's time is not a mechanical, inflexible schedule.
Although the shepherd is wedded to a life "of hope / And
hazard and hard labour" (ll. 253–54), he is nonetheless a
"freeman," and his hard labor is "interchanged / With that
majestic indolence so dear / To native man" (ll. 254–56).

Nature's time is healthful, varied, and flexible in ways
that clock time cannot be; it has its own imperatives, but the
shepherd, being a "freeman," can ignore them. It is when he
does so, liberating himself even from the wholesome rhythm
of nature, that his life yields a particular sweetness and his
human nature is seen to be "Of quality and fabric more divine" than the nature in which he dwells. Wordsworth expresses the matter in a pun of childlike simplicity. When the
shepherd and his dog

                              have stolen,
      As is their wont, a pittance from strict time,
      For rest not needed or exchange of love,
      Then from his couch he starts; and now his feet
      Crush out a livelier fragrance from the flowers
      Of lowly thyme...
                                        (Ll. 238–43)

This moment of "indolence" makes man "majestic" simply
because he alone in his environment is capable of it. And by
defying time he reestablishes the right order of things. "Strict
time" is outer time, of the earth; the mind of man is a
thousand times more beautiful than the earth on which he
dwells. When man asserts his independence, "strict time,"
which offers only a pittance, becomes "lowly thyme," from

which man crushes a "livelier fragrance." This is idleness in the full sense, a willful refusal to follow the suggestions of natural pulses.

Idleness prompted by the spirit of the season is in an important sense not idleness at all. In *The Prelude,* 1:104, Wordsworth describes it as a "Sabbath," and in line 38 of "Ode on Intimations of Immortality," he calls it a "jubilee." Both terms are scriptural, and they have a particular interest in the present context. The sabbath is divinely ordained for man's benefit, its chief purpose being recuperation. The Year of Jubilee was prescribed by Mosaic law, and one of its major provisions was that the land should lie fallow for a year as part of a program for restoring the wealth of Israel (Lev. 25). In Wordsworth's scheme, the idleness of the spirit of the season is, in a strict sense of the word, sabbatical; and it is sanctioned by nature, because, like the Hebrew jubilee, it is necessary for recuperation. But the idleness of the shepherd stealing his pittance from time "For rest not needed" is a significantly different matter. Natural sabbath may be shared by animals and the earth itself; the shepherd's stolen minutes represent a "majestic indolence so dear / To native man" and possible to man alone. In other words, we have now moved from the idleness of the spirit of the season to that of "deliberate holiday," and we are now beginning to be able to see something of that movement through the time schemes that I earlier suggested was a feature of Wordsworth's handling of this theme. Natural sabbath entails a movement from clock time to earth time, and from outer to inner time. Such an advance is healthful and enlightening, leading to stability and moral maturity. But deliberate holiday is even more radical: it asserts man's independence of time altogether, and it does so by defying the limits of all time schemes.

Wordsworth believed that the great moments of illumination and transforming experience followed such periods of idleness. But the idleness has a bliss of its own. In *The Prelude,* 1:59–87, Wordsworth describes a mood of delightful ease following a bout of fervent poetic energy. He is careful to emphasize the deliberateness of his idleness: he is "content and not unwilling" to let his enthusiasm ebb away; he slackens his thoughts "by choice," and settles into "gentler happiness." Sitting beneath a tree on a warm autumn afternoon, ("a day / With silver clouds, and sunshine on the grass") he ponders the question of where to make his home. Finally he decides on a "known Vale" and makes mental images of one particular cottage in it.

> No picture of mere memory ever looked
> So fair; and while upon the fancied scene
> I gazed with growing love, a higher power
> Than Fancy gave assurance of some work
> Of glory there forthwith to be begun,
> Perhaps too there performed. Thus long I mused,
> Nor e'er lost sight of what I mused upon,
> Save when, amid the stately grove of oaks,
> Now here, now there, an acorn, from its cup
> Dislodged, through sere leaves rustled, or at once
> To the bare earth dropped with a startling sound.
> From that soft couch I rose not, till the sun
> Had almost touched the horizon.
>
> (Ll. 75–87)

But this idleness produced more than a decision about where to make his home, and more even than some kind of spiritual assurance about a great work there to be performed. The experience can perhaps be described as a kind of relaxed ecstasy, and the reader needs to look again, very carefully, at all that is going on in the poetry in order to sense the nature of this prolonged joyful absorption.

At first sight the passage appears to be descriptive. But great descriptive poetry usually surprises us with its particularity and astonishing accuracy, as, for example, in Shakespeare's line: "There the snake throws her enamell'd skin." Wordsworth's passage, on the contrary, is conventional and vague, using phrases such as "a green shady place," "silver clouds," and "sunshine on the grass." But this lack of focus does not result from a failure of care or imprecise realization; on the contrary, it is a superior kind of accuracy. The event (and it is an event) which the lines record and recreate is the obliteration of the real world in which Wordsworth is resting by an interior picture, of which Wordsworth cannot be sure whether it is remembered or created. That the interior picture is vivid is expressed by a hint that Wordsworth is going to become particular: "a known Vale;" "the very door," "one cottage." But this implied promise is not fulfilled, and we are coolly told that it cannot be. "No picture of mere memory ever looked / So fair." That is as far as the matter is taken, and that too is as far as it need be taken. The unrealized hints of exactitude are enough to make the imagined scene more real than the roughly crayoned environment. The locale of Wordsworth's trance is a vale and a cottage within his mind, not the sheltered grove in which he is sitting.

The success of the poetry depends on the trancelike state being imposed on, or reproduced in, the reader's mind. To a large extent this effect is achieved rhythmically, through steady, almost undisturbed iambics. But, in spite of the vague impressionism which characterizes the passage, the real power derives from a few carefully placed accuracies which shake us back to wakefulness at precisely the moment when Wordsworth wishes us to become alert. The sun, we are told in lines 66–67, is "two hours declined towards the west." But when we have put our watches back in our pockets, the iambic hypnosis, the visual impressionism, and the softened perceptions conjure the sense of timeless bliss which Wordsworth is determined to promote. For the beauty of the imagined scene is only a part of Wordsworth's joy—the other element is his obliviousness to the passing of the hours. But only through time is time conquered; we only realize that we have had a tremor of bliss when we find ourselves back in the draughty church at smokefall. Hence Wordsworth draws our attention to nature's clocks, which punctuate the timeless happiness with unmistakable observed reality.

Now here, now there, an acorn, from its cup
Dislodged, through sere leaves rustled, or at once
To the bare earth dropped with a startling sound.

Perhaps a clearer picture of the beneficial and creative
kind of idleness emerges if I contrast it with what Wordsworth evidently thought of as its polar opposite, the utilitarian, regulated ceaseless striving of the Gradgrind school-
room.

These mighty workmen of our later age,
Who, with a broad highway, have overbridged
The froward chaos of futurity,
Tamed to their bidding; they who have the skill
To manage books, and things, and make them act
On infant minds as surely as the sun
Deals with a flower; the keepers of our time,
The guides and wardens of our faculties,
Sages who in their prescience would control
All accidents, and to the very road
Which they have fashioned would confine us down,
Like engines; when will their presumption learn,
That in the unreasoning progress of the world
A wiser spirit is at work for us,
A better eye than theirs, most prodigal
Of blessings, and most studious of our good,
Even in what seem our most unfruitful hours?
(*Prelude,* 5:347–63)

The youthful Wordsworth was a revolutionary in a very
wide sense. These lines express radical criticism of the educational methods and aims of his day and of the social and
cultural values associated with them. The poet is attacking
something more fundamental than officious, tidy-minded
schoolmasters; the real evil is the hubris that assumes con-
temporary values to be self-validating and eternal and so
leads to the indoctrination of the young rather than to their
education. One of the things the Romantic movement was

rebelling against was the scientific optimism of the seven-
teenth and eighteenth centuries that held, sometimes with the
naivete of Bishop Thomas Sprat, one of the founders of the
Royal Society and the author of a history of it (1667), that the
natural world would soon be fully understood and controlled, the sooner if men would keep emotion and metaphor
under strict discipline. People of this cast of mind will have
things tidy, will "manage books, and things," "control all
accidents," "confine us down, / Like engines," and, when
we go to their school, the first thing they will ask us to learn
is the class timetable. People who will be "keepers of our
time" will be keepers of much else. And the frightening thing
is the plasticity of the material such pedagogues work upon.
Can we imagine the educationists Wordsworth is attacking
ever suffering a tremor of self-doubt or an instant's self-
examination at the contemplation of a youthful mind that, as
Gerard Manley Hopkins puts it, "to all I teach / Yields tender
as a pushed peach"? The ready acceptance of teaching by the
young will seem to the complacent and myopic teacher to
certify the rightness of what is taught; such a teacher will act
on infant minds "as surely as the sun deals with a flower."
Wordsworth in this image of sun and flower deliberately
emphasizes that the teaching and learning processes are
natural, but canker and blight are also natural processes, and
lilies that fester smell far worse than weeds.

A little earlier in *The Prelude,* Wordsworth presents a
picture of the ideal product of this educational method in a
passage that deserves more attention than it usually gets. The
poet's drift in the following lines may not be obvious, but it
is not obscure; he is trying to show the effects of a young life
so thoroughly organized according to a principle of perpetual
utilitarian hard work that it allows no scope for any kind of
idleness, and therefore no scope for mental spontaneity,
curiosity, or wonderment.

                         that common sense
        May try this modern system by its fruits,

Leave let me take to place before her sight
A specimen pourtrayed with faithful hand.
Full early trained to worship seemliness,
This model of a child is never known
To mix in quarrels; that were far beneath
Its dignity; with gifts he bubbles o'er
As generous as a fountain; selfishness
May not come near him, nor the little throng
Of flitting pleasures tempt him from his path;
The wandering beggars propagate his name,
Dumb creatures find him tender as a nun,
And natural or supernatural fear,
Unless it leap upon him in a dream,
Touches him not. To enhance the wonder, see
How arch his notices, how nice his sense
Of the ridiculous; nor blind is he
To the broad follies of the licensed world,
Yet innocent himself withal, though shrewd,
And can read lectures upon innocence;
A miracle of scientific lore,
Ships he can guide across the pathless sea,
And tell you all their cunning; he can read
The inside of the earth, and spell the stars;
He knows the policies of foreign lands;
Can string you names of districts, cities, towns,
The whole world over, tight as beads of dew
Upon a gossamer thread; he sifts, he weighs;
All things are put to question; he must live
Knowing that he grows wiser every day
Or else not live at all, and seeing too
Each little drop of wisdom as it falls
Into the dimpling cistern of his heart;
For this unnatural growth the trainer blame,
Pity the tree.—Poor human vanity,
Wert thou extinguished, little would be left
Which he could truly love; but how escape?

(*Prelude*, 5:294–331)

Wordsworth does not often demand attention as an ironist,
but this passage not only has an interest for my purpose, it

also has merit. It is not irony of a high order (it lacks, for
example, the subtly graduated ambivalence of Marvell's
"Horatian Ode"), but it has the essential unity of good satire,
the judgment is in the manner, and there is a fine control of
rhythm, emphasis, and tone. The invitation to apply common sense to the matter in hand is made in the straightforward language of common sense, but the burlesque of pedan-
try begins immediately with the Latinist inversion of "Leave
let us take" and the fussy grandiloquence of "to place before
her sight." The attitude the reader is to take to the well-
educated child is unmistakable in the botanical note struck by
"A specimen." In the next line, "Full early trained to worship
seemliness," is both a Drydenesque satirical bathos and a
deadly pun—the alumnus of this college knows the value of
appearances. While there are several possible understandings
of "this model of a child," all but one are pejorative, and the
only admirable application is pulled up short at the line-end
pause, "is never known." The verb in "that were far
beneath / Its dignity" is an almost sneering subjunctive, and
the rhythmically maneuvered emphasis on "dignity" makes
that precocious dignity ridiculous. All the artificiality so far
suggested ensures that the fountain in the next lines is seen as
one contrived by man, where the showering waters are collected in the concrete basin and returned to the pump
chamber. The implication is pointed by the word "selfishness," held back momentarily from the verb of which it is the
subject. The paragon knows no "little throng" either of pleasures, or, one suspects, playmates. Yet his virtues are the
ones we approve after all—he is kind to dumb animals and
gives alms to the poor. But in case one misses the point of the
fountain image, that all his virtues flow inwards to replenish
his self-esteem, there is another hint: "The wandering beggars propagate his name." There is a jibe in "propagate." The
boy's virtues only perform their ego-nourishing function,
when, as Shakespeare's Ulysses suggests to Achilles, "he be-
holds them framed in the applause." Furthermore, this virtue
is not merely ingrowing, it is also spurious. The character so

built up by education is "not blind" to the "licensed world,"
but he does not live in it nor even near enough to see it
clearly. Vice is not within tempting distance. He can read
lectures upon innocence, but this innocence is that cloistered
virtue that neither Milton nor Wordsworth praise.

The academic learning of this child is equally a simula-
crum. "Ships he can guide across the pathless sea," but so
could W. S. Gilbert's Sir Joseph Porter, who stuck close to
his desk and never went to sea. He "spells" rather than sees
the stars; he does not wonder at them. His knowledge is a
collection of theories and a catalogue of names which he can
string "tight as beads of dew / Upon a gossamer thread"—a
structure which, if the least brush with common reality does
not shatter, the heat of the day will evaporate. His learning is
prompted by the same regard as his virtue.

> He must live
> Knowing that he grows wiser every day,
> Or else not live at all.

What wisdom is there in such motivation? And such wisdom
as he distills is collected in the "cistern" of his heart. At
examination times he merely opens the valve.

Not the least remarkable quality of this passage is its
prophetic nature. Wordsworth asks what would remain of
such a boy's education, once bereft of the induced conceit
that prompted it.

> Poor human vanity,
> Wert thou extinguished, little would be left
> Which he could truly love; but how escape?

How cruelly apposite this is to our modern pressure system
of social status and academic prestige, institutionalized and
venerated, from school examinations to the classified honors
degree.

The symbol and symptom of all that I have been discuss-
ing in these passages is the phrase "the keepers of our time."

The class timetable, crammed full of what is significantly called "work," is the emblem of all that is so offensively tidy-minded and doctrinaire in the education provided by a so-called good school, particularly a good nineteenth-century British school. In such a school only the perpetually busy student will win approval, and idleness will be regarded as the sin second only to erotism in moral odium, and no doubt connected with it. That there can be a kind of idleness which is fruitful, or conducive to self-knowledge, is an idea which will either never be entertained, or, if acknowledged, will immediately be subordinated to the demands of the syllabus, and the need for "getting on."

In these respects school is, in a horribly real sense, a preparation for life. Few of us enjoy the confidence of a Raisley Calvert (who bequeathed Wordsworth nine hundred pounds), and fewer still deserve it. For most of us life is a schedule. There is an implicit case for idleness, then, in the passage I have been examining. To know ourselves, to win some sense of moral orientation in the world we find ourselves part of, it may be necessary deliberately to ignore the schedule, to do as we like for a while, or to do nothing but look and listen, to be idle in fact. But Wordsworth in *The Prelude* is not only concerned with this general case, he is concerned with the development of his own creative power, and for this it is sometimes necessary to defy more than the social time scheme. In *The Prelude,* 1:425–63, Wordsworth handles the time images more adroitly than in any passage of *The Prelude* I have yet discussed, and the deliberateness of his disobedience of all time's commands is fully explicit.

> And in the frosty season, when the sun
> Was set, and visible for many a mile
> The cottage windows blazed through twilight gloom,
> I heeded not their summons: happy time
> It was indeed for all of us—for me
> It was a time of rapture! Clear and loud
> The village clock tolled six,—I wheeled about,

Proud and exulting like an untired horse
That cares not for his home. All shod with steel,
We hissed along the polished ice in games
Confederate, imitative of the chase
And woodland pleasures,—the resounding horn,
The pack loud chiming, and the hunted hare.
So through the darkness and the cold we flew,
And not a voice was idle; with the din
Smitten, the precipices rang aloud;
The leafless trees and every icy crag
Tinkled like iron; while far distant hills
Into the tumult sent an alien sound
Of melancholy not unnoticed, while the stars
Eastward were sparkling clear, and in the west
The orange sky of evening died away.
Not seldom from the uproar I retired
Into a silent bay, or sportively
Glanced sideway, leaving the tumultuous throng,
To cut across the reflex of a star
That fled, and, flying still before me, gleamed
Upon the glassy plain; and oftentimes,
When we had given our bodies to the wind,
And all the shadowy banks on either side
Came sweeping through the darkness, spinning still
The rapid line of motion, then at once
Have I, reclining back upon my heels,
Stopped short; yet still the solitary cliffs
Wheeled by me—even as if the earth had rolled
With visible motion her diurnal round!
Behind me did they stretch in solemn train,
Feebler and feebler, and I stood and watched
Till all was tranquil as a dreamless sleep.

This passage begins with a peculiarly Wordsworthian kind of
ambiguity, the kind of doubleness of understanding that
amounts to a brilliantly economical accuracy. In lines 425–26,
the iambic momentum that carries the reader over the
comma after "set" and the line-end pause that makes him
hesitate after "mile" together produce the notion that the sun

was set and yet visible for miles around. The effect of this is that commonsense resolutions of the paradox—the idea that the sun is set in that its lower rim has passed below the skyline, or that it is fully set in the valleys but still visible from the mountain slopes, or, finally, that it is indeed set, but that the fiery glow is still visible for many a mile—all these almost instantaneously spring to mind, and Wordsworth has deftly and immediately defined the period of evening with which the passage is concerned. He has also compounded the two time schemes, human and natural, by the simple device of making the syntactically accurate reading follow instantly and obviously: "The cottage windows blazed through twilight gloom." And by sheer proximity, "blazed" seems to make contact with "the sun / Was set and visible" and also with "twilight," while "gloom" by contrast suggests the darker sides of the fells and sheltered bays of the lake. All the ambiguities are cross-fertilizing and contribute to definition rather than vagueness. The point Wordsworth has thus ingeniously made is that this is precisely the period when the time schemes conflict; it is, after all, the cottage windows that blaze and are visible for many a mile, and the young skaters cannot fail to see them.

"I heeded not their summons." The note struck by this line is pride, not contrition. Moreover, Wordsworth is not trying to excuse the disobedience in "happy time / It was indeed for all of us—for me / It was a time of rapture." One is left uncertain whether the summons was unheeded because of the rapture or the rapture experienced because the summons was ignored. Wordsworth uses no limiting "because" or "thus." Nevertheless, he allows no mistake about the willfulness of his defiance.

> Clear and loud
> The village clock tolled six,—I wheeled about
> Proud and exulting like an untired horse
> That cares not for his home.

The time is absolutely specific: the clock has struck six. The disobedience is dramatic and obvious. Wordsworth "wheeled about," and the mood is not merely "proud and exulting," but that of the rogue animal "that cares not for his home."

These lines make the most fully explicit statement of the matter, but the commands of time and the defiance of the children are reiterated implicitly over and over again. The chimes of the clock, modulated by mountain echoes perhaps, are heard in "resounding horn," "pack loud chiming," "din / Smitten," "rang aloud," and "tinkled like iron." But the game of hare and hounds goes on—the echoing tones of time's authority are mischievously absorbed into it by the onomatopoeia. Nevertheless, the echo itself obtrudes into the happiness, and in the margin of their consciousness the children sadly note the claims of the clock. The chime is a social, artificial signal, foreign to the holiday time of nature, and its echoes begin to subvert the wild pleasure.

> far distant hills
> Into the tumult sent an alien sound
> Of melancholy not unnoticed, while the stars
> Eastward were sparkling clear, and in the west
> The orange sky of evening died away.

When the last light of sunset has failed, nature too calls a halt; the blending of the echoing bells into the natural scheme and the skaters' tumult reminds one that what the mechanical clock records is the turning of the earth. The chimes of six mean, among other things, that it will soon be dark and then the games must stop.

Wordsworth, however, does not stop. After the "orange sky of evening" has died away, we see him alone, retired from the uproar, which suggests that he, more daring than the rest, defies even nature's time limits. And by an uncommonly adroit image the poetry suggests that his effort is to catch up on time, to keep pace with the circling sky.

> To cut across the reflex of a star
> That fled, and flying still before me, gleamed
> Upon the glassy plain.

One cannot be sure whether Wordsworth is alone or not, for he says, "When we had given our bodies to the wind." But the special visionary experience is his alone.

>   at once
> Have I, reclining back upon my heels,
> Stopped short; yet still the solitary cliffs
> Wheeled by me—even as if the earth had rolled
> With visible motion her diurnal round.

It is his alone because he alone has defied even nature's time. The notion of deliberate holiday detaches itself quite clearly from the notion of natural sabbath. And what is gained by this defiance of time is of a higher order than what is gained by responding to the spirit of the season. In this instance Wordsworth seems to see the earth-clock working, "the great globe itself" rotating. Presumably he is actually experiencing a kind of giddiness, the little spirit levels in the ear being disturbed by the sharp deceleration. But for Wordsworth, it is a visionary sensation, a seeing time itself in movement. And this "seeing into the life of things" is the direct and immediate reward of Wordsworth's defiance of time. The rapture of deliberate holiday approaches, at its most intense, a kind of liberation from time, a momentary conviction of the ultimate independence of the mind from time's processes.

    This is perhaps a good point at which to deal with two difficulties which many people nowadays experience in reading Wordsworth's accounts of these moments of insight. First, the experiences often seem to be based merely on an error of perception. For example, the mountain that strode after him and the moon dropping so swiftly behind Lucy's cottage roof seem to indicate simply Wordsworth's naive failure to realize how movement alters the horizon. In the present instance the mistake is a little more understandable— the boy Wordsworth could hardly be expected to know the neurology of the matter. All the same, the reader knows, and for some readers the knowledge seems to make the whole passage suspect, both as literature and as a document of mystical experience. If the experience was a sham, the poetry becomes a kind of sham, farcically presenting not Wordsworth the visionary boy, but Wordsworth the duffer.

The second difficulty arises from the fact that the experiences are mystical and therefore seem to have religious implications. Current habits of thought being what they are, many critics now feel that they ought to identify some secularized meaning or psychological diagnosis of which a modern reader may approve. Consequently much ink is spilled in explaining away the moments of vision or in trying to demonstrate that Wordsworth didn't really believe what the poetry seems to imply. All such argumentation is worse than a waste of time, because it involves a falsification of the experiences Wordsworth is celebrating. We must take the poetry for what it really is, and we can do so without being embarrassed by the mysticism. The supposed difficulties about the origins and nature of all such experiences are in fact irrelevant, as William James made clear in his introductory Gifford Lecture at the University of Edinburgh in 1901.

> In recent books of logic, distinction is made between two orders of inquiry concerning anything. First, what is the nature of it? How did it come about? What is its constitution, origin, and history? And second, what is its _importance_, meaning or significance, now that it is once here? The answer to the one question is given in an *existential* judgment or proposition. The answer to the other is a *proposition of value,* what the Germans call a *Werthurtheil,* or what we may, if we like, denominate a *spiritual judgment.* Neither can be deduced immediately from the other. They proceed from diverse intellectual preoccupations. . . .
> Medical materialism finishes up St Paul by calling his

vision on the road to Damascus a discharging lesion of the
occipital cortex, he being an epileptic. It snuffs out St Teresa
as an hysteric, St Francis of Assisi as an hereditary degenerate.
George Fox's discontent with the shams of his age, and his
pining for spiritual veracity, it treats as symptoms of a disordered colon. . . .
    Let us play fair with this whole matter, and be quite
candid with ourselves and with the facts. When we think
certain states of mind superior to others, is it ever because of
what we know concerning their organic antecedents? No! It is
always for two entirely different reasons. It is either because
we take an immediate delight in them; or else it is because we
believe them to bring us good consequential fruits for
life. . . . It is the character of inner happiness in the thoughts
which stamps them as good, or else their consistency with our
other opinions and their serviceability for our needs which
make them pass for true in our esteem.[3]

James's field was psychology; he was therefore concerned with the value of a condition of mind, rather than
with the truth of a set of beliefs. Medical materialism may
very well show us that willful idleness, a conscious rejection
of the demands of the schedule, predispose the mind and
nerves to pleasant sensations of an almost intoxicated inten-
sity, much akin to the experiences described in the writings
of religious mystics. It doesn't matter. What matters is "the
good consequential fruit" which such experiences had for the
mind of a poet.
    There remain two further points of Wordsworthian
guile to note before leaving this passage. Wordsworth has
only said "*as if* the earth had rolled." Our first readings tend
to slide over the phrase, as if it were merely a part of the
hissing skates onomatopoeia. But the adult poet is in charge,
in spite of the boy's momentary delusion. And again, the
sense in which seeing the earth turning may be called a delusion is a curious one, because after "medical materialism" has
finished explaining about nerve centers and the canals of the
inner ear and so forth, the poet can still mutter, with Galileo,

"It does move all the same." The delusion consists in seeming to see what does really happen, when in the nature of things it cannot be seen. We can here add another validation of the mystical moment: we may be deceived by our senses, but the deception may be entirely consonant with reality. The reality which Wordsworth has seen here is the mathematical continuum, realized in the imagination, not deduced from the observation of relative motion. And the moment of seeing is accompanied by spiritual calm, tranquil as a dreamless sleep.

Such moments are not always so accompanied. Occasionally the mystical experience pertains to the "ministry of fear" and is attended by panic and a persisting sense of "unknown modes of being." It may be significant, too, that one of the most famous of these chastening moments is produced by enforced rather than deliberate holiday. Riding from the family home towards Penrith, the young Wordsworth became separated from his guide. Alone, he came upon a place where a murder had been committed and the murderer had been executed for his crime.

> through fear
> Dismounting, down the rough and stony moor
> I led my horse, and, stumbling on, at length
> Came to a bottom, where in former times
> A murderer had been hung in iron chains.
> The gibbet-mast had mouldered down, the bones
> And iron case were gone; but on the turf,
> Hard by, soon after that fell deed was wrought,
> Some unknown hand had carved the murderer's name.
> The monumental letters were inscribed
> In times long past; but still, from year to year,
> By superstition of the neighbourhood,
> The grass is cleared away, and to this hour
> The characters are fresh and visible:
> A casual glance had shown them, and I fled,
> Faltering and faint, and ignorant of the road:
> Then, reascending the bare common, saw

A naked pool that lay beneath the hills,
The beacon on the summit, and, more near,
A girl, who bore a pitcher on her head,
And seemed with difficult steps to force her way
Against the blowing wind. It was, in truth,
An ordinary sight; but I should need
Colours and words that are unknown to man,
To paint the visionary dreariness
Which, while I looked all round for my lost guide,
Invested moorland waste, and naked pool,
The beacon crowning the lone eminence,
The female and her garments vexed and tossed
By the strong wind. When, in the blessed hours
Of early love, the loved one at my side,
I roamed, in daily presence of this scene,
Upon the naked pool and dreary crags,
And on the melancholy beacon fell
A spirit of pleasure and youth's golden gleam.

                                            (*Prelude,* 12:232–66)

This passage is full of verbal and syntactical cunning, but the
key words, "fear" and "invested," are prominently placed.
The incident happened when Wordsworth was very young
and still a very inexperienced horseman. Having "by some
mischance" become "disjoined" from the servant who was
supposed to be taking care of him, he is naturally frightened.
He dismounts simply because he knows he will be safer on
foot. The mere fact of being separated from his guardian,
however, continues to be a cause of fear, and the small boy is
soon in a mood to be frightened by anything. The "visionary
dreariness" may be seen as a projection onto the natural environment of the terror and bewilderment in the child's mind,
which Wordsworth virtually acknowledges by his use of the
word "invested." Add to this the fact that the already
frightened boy comes across an old gibbet and a murderer's
name carved in the turf, and the whole affair becomes a psy-
chologist's textbook case, illustrating the mind's capacity to
project its moods onto the environment. The medical judg-

ment is undoubtedly accurate, and I need not bother to dispute it. But I am concerned with another kind of judgment, neither existential in James's sense nor spiritual, but literary and critical.

One of the most striking features of the passage is its capacity to make the reader see by glimpses—out of the corner of his eye—things that are either not there or that disappear when he turns a direct view on them. There is, for instance, the rotting body of the murderer: "The gibbet mast had mouldered down, the bones . . . " Ambiguity contrived by alternative punctuation is a familiar device.[4] The rhythm encouraged by the line-end pause makes "bones" a direct object of "mouldered down," which is at first read as a transitive verb. The body is still there, corrupted it seems by the very gibbet on which it hangs. But the true predicate of the clause becomes apparent in the next line: "the bones / And iron case were gone." And so is the hallucination. The device is not merely familiar, it is ancient, and we can trace it back at least as far as *Ralph Roister Doister*. In this play by Nicholas Udall, Mathew Merygreeke causes confusion by reading Ralph's love letter to Mistress Custance entirely according to the rhythmic punctuation of line-end pauses: "Sweet mistress, whereas I love you nothing at all, / Regarding your substance and richesse chief of all, / For your personage," and so on. When the Scrivener rereads the letter to the hapless Ralph, he restores the syntactical punctuation: "Sweet mistress, whereas I love you, nothing at all / Regarding your richesse and substance: chief of all / For your personage. . . ." Wordsworth, of course, uses the trick more subtly than Udall and for a much more dramatic purpose.

The serious pun is also a traditional device. In line 240, the word "monumental" means both "huge like a monument" and "used as a memorial." But Wordsworth has added a doubleness of tone, for monuments are usually memorials of respect and not, as in this case, horror. And this pun economically introduces the time theme—the sense of the persistence of evil in the place in which it occurred. The

murderer's name remains vividly legible. But it does so because someone's hands carefully clear away the grass that
would, in the way of nature, grow over it. The persistence is
not in fact supernatural; there are no ghosts. It obtains in the
minds of men determined to perpetuate both the deed and
society's revenge. Yet one does for an instant see ghosts,
perpetually enacting whatever passionate or ritual barbarity
the gibbet now commemorates, an eternally repetitive spec-
tral drama, and this chilling glimpse is made possible by
another serious but seemingly careless pun, this time on the
word "characters."

> to this hour
> The characters are fresh and visible:
> A casual glance had shown them, and I fled.

If the child could view the rotting gibbet without panic, it is
not obvious why the sight of the name should put him to
flight. It is probable, since the execution took place in 1767,
that the young Wordsworth had heard the whole tale, in
which case the name would involve a horrified recognition.
The realization that he was on the very spot where both the
murder and the retribution took place might well induce
panic. But the reader needs a certain amount of time, and
perhaps the help of de Selincourt's editorial notes, to understand the lines in this way. More immediate is the notion of
spiritually evil "characters" visibly present, glimpsed by accident in the margin of vision. This is the immediate and
sufficient motive for "I fled." If the passage is read in this
way, "reascending the bare common" has, as well as its geo-
graphical meaning, a sense of struggling back to normal consciousness and normal conditions of perception, but still with
supernatural fear obsessing the mind and making it ready to
"invest" the "common" with hostile spiritual qualities. Thus
the "ordinary sight" of the common and the girl with the
pitcher on her head becomes indescribably desolate and
menacing—a "visionary dreariness." But here I am merely

making existential judgments, while the judgment of value must emerge from an analysis of the manner in which Wordsworth creates the visionary dreariness. Unquestionably he does create it; our experience of the passage is, in Coleridge's phrase, "analogous to the supernatural." Much of this sense of the supernatural derives from our immediate recall of the momentary ghostly visions near the gibbet, but there is yet something more, something in the features Wordsworth has chosen to note, that sets off weird reverberations. The beacon, for instance, ought to be reassuring, it is so definite a landmark. But to see it thus requires more self-discipline than the terrified child can muster, and it attracts to itself the evil associations of the gibbet. The girl is a real human person—human aid and reassurance is available and near at hand. But she now has some of the ghostly qualities of the "characters" seen in the terrible hollow; she is thus distanced and put out of reach. From the human nearness of "girl" she recedes to "female," whose garments are "vexed and tossed." In general the dreariness of the landscape is the dreariness of a moor in late autumn or early winter, and this, superficially, is the signification of the bleak epithets: "bare common," "naked pool," "moorland waste," "lone eminence," "blowing wind," and so on. But the female figure remains a challenge. Why is she so strong a catalyst to the menacing processes engendered by the imagery and the epithets? She is certainly not mentioned simply because she happened to be there, like Matthew's bough of wilding. She stirs uneasy memories, and we cannot be sure what it is we are remembering. The pitcher on her head suggests a biblical figure—the wanton of Samaria perhaps, going to the well. Or is she the murderer's victim, or the murderer herself perhaps? It is known, of course, who the murderer was, and who his victim. In Cowdrake Quarry near Penrith Beacon, Thomas Nicholson murdered Thomas Parker, for which crime Nicholson was executed and his dead body hung in chains in the quarry. But these facts do not invalidate the point I made about the female with the pitcher. In the terrified consciousness of the boy, she may be the specter of some "character" associated with the murder. The facts of the case form only the starting point of poetic treatment. And we know that Wordsworth did not in other respects stick to the facts. The letters carved in the turf, for example, were simply "T. P. M.," signifying "Thomas Parker murdered," and not the murderer's name.

It is also possible to see the female in a less hostile light. She may not be an embodiment of evil sensed in the environment; she may in fact be the struggling human personality, carrying her burden and performing her necessary task in the teeth of the wind that would pluck away the human sophistication of clothes, leaving an "unaccommodated being," "naked," "bare," and "lone" as the country she traverses, or that would defeat her altogether and make her retrace her steps. For she is herself buffeted by the wind, for the text reads "The female and her garments vexed and tossed / By the strong wind." This is a Dantesque wind, blowing before and after time. But whether she embodies evil or the heroic soul beset by evil and enduring purgatory, she is distant, "female," depersonalized, and unapproachable, and hence the contrast of the whole experience to the daily visits to the scene later in Wordsworth's life, "the loved one at my side." It is not merely the presence of Mary Hutchinson but the state of mind of Wordsworth happy in love that invests the scene with the spirit of pleasure. The "auxiliar light" of the mind is variable, since it is not a purely intellectual light. It is a light that derives from the personality as a whole, from memory, glands, and nerve endings, as well as from the cerebral cortex. The importance of this auxiliar light is its power to transmute outward objects, to make the same neutral world one either of "visionary dreariness" or of "youth's golden gleam." And besides being the source of the auxiliar light, the mind is the seat of the will. The time theme of this passage is basically a conflict between nature's tendency to bury the dead and man's willful determination to keep his vengeance aflame. Nature would forget the murderer's name, but unforgiving human hands keep the letters tidily legible, perpetuating evil. The change in the look of the place in the last lines of the passage is a change wrought by love. I should note one thing more. Wordsworth experienced the sense of "visionary dreariness" during an enforced departure from the schedule of daily life, but he experienced the vision of the dreary land transfigured during what is, for the common man, the most blessed kind of deliberate holiday, the enchanted idleness of courtship.

6

Spots of Time and the Weight of Ages

Wordsworth uses the expression "spots of time" to describe only two specific occasions: the Cowdrake Quarry incident (*Prelude,* 12:225–66) and the period of waiting for the coach to take him home for the Christmas holidays during which his father died (*Prelude,* 12:287–335). Nevertheless, the expression is clearly applicable to many of the other moments of mystical apprehension, including the moments of visionary joy as well as these two moments of visionary dreariness. The words suggest moments which have a perceptible separateness from the general flow of time, a suggestion strengthened by the quality Wordsworth attributes to these moments—"distinct pre-eminence" (*Prelude,* 12:209). As David Perkins has pointed out, "freezing" the moment is an artistic necessity.

Anyone who contemplates his own thoughts and feelings finds that they are always in process, changing as they recombine with different elements. Even our past is not settled, but constantly assumes new shapes and meanings in the shifting lights of the present. Yet a poem only can exist by solidifying a moment in the flux of consciousness.[1]

And yet I am not quite happy with the manner in which Perkins expresses the idea. "Solidifying a moment in the flux" has certain unfortunate undertones: if this is what poetry does, and all it does, it would seem to be a kind of imaginative thrombosis. William F. Lynch has very effectively attacked the notion that the function of art is to freeze some moment of the past, "so that we may have it for ever, and thus share in that quality of eternity that does not move but simply *is*. . . . The impulse itself represents a disease of the feelings."[2] Lynch is surely right, and the sickness he diagnoses is that which Keats struggles against in "Ode on a Grecian Urn": "Forever wilt thou love, and she be fair!" The real power of Wordsworth's moments is not their frozenness or their solidity, but the immense energy within them, their power to make the reader's imagination work backward and forward in an instant. And indeed, the very phrase "spots of time" and Wordsworth's frequent use of the term "moments" suggest that he actually senses these moments, not as a solidifying of the flux, but as in a sense not part of the flux at all.

It is possible that Wordsworth had absorbed in some form the Cartesian notion of the discontinuity of time. This doctrine is worth looking at briefly, since there is a sense in which it fits Wordsworth's apparent assumptions about the nature of his mystical moments. At a certain point in the Third Meditation, Descartes is concerned with the "false infinite"—the idea, that is, of an endless series of second causes. Such a series would eliminate the need for a first cause and thus go far towards denying the existence of God. Descartes rejects the notion on the ground that, while it may account for the origin of being, it does not account for persistence in being.

For the whole duration of human life is divisible into count-
less parts, all mutually independent; so from my having
existed a little while ago it does not follow that I need exist
now, unless some cause creates me anew at this very moment,
in other words, preserves me. For it is clear, when one considers the nature of time, that just the same power and agency
is needed to preserve any object at the various moments of its
duration, as would be needed to create it anew if it did not yet
exist; there is thus only a conceptual distinction between pres-
ervation and creation, and this is one of the things that are
obvious by the light of nature.[3]

Time is discrete, then, an infinite series of separate moments,
and objects endure by virtue of an infinite series of separate
acts of conservation by God. These separate moments would
not form a succession if God did not hold them together by a
continuous act of creation. This is one of the many points
where Descartes's thought appears paradoxical. He seems to
be saying that God sustains the world by an infinite series of
separate acts of conservation and at the same time that God's
action is continuous. But what God is doing *continuously* is
creating *discontinuous* moments. The effect is that the created
world will appear to endure continuously, though in reality
its moments are discontinuous.[4] A motion picture film provides a rough-and-ready analogy. The film is not chopped
up; it is a continuous strip of separate frames. The effect of
the film running through the projector is to produce the illusion of continuous, not discontinuous, action. But the separateness, the discreteness, is the reality.

At the risk of doing an injustice to Descartes, let me take
the film analogy a little further. If I am watching a film and
the projector stops on a single frame, what kind of thing
happens in my mind? Of course I become aware of the picture as a picture, rather than as an instant in an unfolding
action, and its details become available to me in a way they
are not when in action. But at the same time I am aware that
the projector has stopped, and thereby I become aware of the
existence of a projector and film in a way I was not aware of

them while the film was in motion. I become aware of the discrete nature of the images. I become aware of the reality of discreteness, in fact, which produces the illusion of continuity. And when I read one of Wordsworth's passages dealing with his visionary experiences, I am aware of a temporal context for the stilled moment as I am not for the "moment" pictured on the Grecian urn. (Keats has, of course, "frozen" and "solidified" his picture for a very special purpose. Readers' minds work backwards and forwards between the urn and the poet himself; the marble men and maidens have no before and after.) What one perceives in Wordsworth's moments, however, is not a solidifying or freezing of the process, but an awareness, a sudden and unusual awareness, of discreteness. When one of these supreme moments singles itself out, Wordsworth becomes aware of the sensuous detail of the visible world in a heightened way, but he also feels that he knows reality, that such moments are moments of knowing, and that normal consciousness is, in a sense, a necessary state of illusion. And his verse describing these moments always implies that he has a special kind of awareness of the reality and unity of the universe, that the effects of the moment are beneficial and lasting, and that the experience is in fact sacramental. Time stops, but the value lies not in the oddity of time stopping, but in the reality thus made available, the seeing into the life of things.

The passage in *The Prelude,* 12:208–24 is quite explicit about this question of value.

> There are in our existence spots of time,
> That with distinct pre-eminence retain
> A renovating virtue, whence, depressed
> By false opinion and contentious thought,
> Or ought of heavier or more deadly weight,
> In trivial occupations, and the round
> Of ordinary intercourse, our minds
> Are nourished and invisibly repaired;
> A virtue, by which pleasure is enhanced,
> That penetrates, enables us to mount,

When high, more high, and lifts us up when fallen.
This efficacious spirit chiefly lurks
Among those passages of life that give
Profoundest knowledge to what point, and how,
The mind is lord and master—outward sense
The obedient servant of her will. Such moments
Are scattered everywhere.

William James, in the defense of mystical experience I quoted earlier, makes the point that one of the reasons we hold certain states of mind and certain kinds of experience to be valuable is that they have "good consequential fruits for life." Wordsworth seems to be saying the same sort of thing in the phrase "renovating virtue." The moments of vision, whether accompanied by deep tranquility, as in the skating episode, or by supernatural terror, as in the incident at Cowdrake Quarry, all contribute to that "calm existence that is mine when I / Am worthy of myself" (*Prelude*, 1:350–51). But the "renovating virtue" reappears in line 219 as an "efficacious spirit," and "lurks / Among... passages of life." Certainly Wordsworth is not suggesting a spirit in the sense of an angelic being who visits him on these occasions, but he was probably content to allow the suggestion of this interpretation to float about the surface of meaning, since although his chief subject is the moral refreshment yielded by these moments, this renovation is a by-product of a mystical insight, a sense of a creating, sustaining, and harmonizing power present in nature. A necessary predisposition for these insights is a state of being in which we are most conscious of the supremacy of the human mind and of the mind's lordship over material things (ll. 220–23). The same point is made, even more explicitly perhaps, in lines 41–49 of "Tintern Abbey," where Wordsworth describes

that serene and blessed mood,
In which the affections gently lead us on,—
Until, the breath of this corporeal frame
And even the motion of our human blood

> Almost suspended, we are laid asleep
> In body, and become a living soul:
>   . . . . .
> We see into the life of things.

We see the nature of the reality that is other than our own
mind at the very moment when we are most aware of the
nature of our own mind; the mystical act of knowing is also
an act of self-knowing. And once we have seen what the
mind is, of what, and to what extent it is lord and master, we
achieve a certain moral and emotional stability; we cannot be
easily swayed from our beliefs and moral habits, and we are
not unusually depressed by the weary business of ordinary
routine, by the malice or sneers of other people. The lines
from *The Prelude* recall a similar statement in lines 123–33 of
"Tintern Abbey."

> neither evil tongues,
> Rash judgments, nor the sneers of selfish men,
> Nor greetings where no kindness is, nor all
> The dreary intercourse of daily life,
> Shall e'er prevail against us, or disturb
> Our cheerful faith . . .

Even if the world does begin to oppress us, our minds
may be "invisibly repaired"—the "Tintern Abbey" lines
promise "tranquil restoration." The spots of time become
part of the store of memories available for our healing, for
another aspect of the dignity of the mind is its power of
selective and disciplined memory. We can, at need, recall the
visionary moment. What we felt we may no longer com-
mand, but how we felt we can remember; our spirits can turn
to the sylvan Wye for those sweet sensations and their
spiritual therapy.

These moments, then, are brief glimpses of a kind of
reality normally hidden from us, and their value for us is that
through them, and through our memories of them, we
achieve a degree of spiritual self-possession, a moral sobriety,

an ability to remain undisturbed by whatever is frivolous, hysterical, or merely fashionable. What is gained, in fact, is a fundamental and invulnerable peace of mind, a conviction that, as T. S. Eliot says in the last lines of "Little Gidding," "all shall be well . . . when the fire and the rose are one." There will always be those among Wordsworth's readers who will see such confidence as self-deception, a retreat to the essential snugness of "snug Anglicanism."[5] With this line of thought, of course, goes the assumption that retreat is always cowardly and never wise; the possibility is not entertained that a mystical retreat may be a falling back *pour mieux sauter.* But in Wordsworth's scheme we are not encouraged to resort to mysticism as if it were a stupefying drug, for the reverence for the human mind that these moments necessarily inspire includes reverence for the mind's capacity for "right reason," which naturally directs us to the business of living in the present world.

> I had been taught to reverence a Power
> That is the visible quality and shape
> And image of right reason; that matures
> Her processes by steadfast laws; gives birth
> To no impatient or fallacious hopes,
> No heat of passion or excessive zeal,
> No vain conceits; provokes to no quick turns
> Of self-applauding intellect; but trains
> To meekness, and exalts by humble faith;
> Holds up before the mind intoxicate
> With present objects, and the busy dance
> Of things that pass away, a temperate show
> Of objects that endure; and by this course
> Disposes her, when over-fondly set
> On throwing off incumbrances, to seek
> In man, and in the frame of social life,
> Whate'er there is desirable and good
> Of kindred permanence, unchanged in form
> And function, or, through strict vicissitude
> Of life and death, revolving.
>
> (*Prelude,* 13:20–39)

All of Wordsworth's spots of time have in common the qualities I have identified. But individually they have other characteristics whereby they may be distinguished. For while they all are moments of knowing, sometimes in a decidedly gnostic sense, the thing known is often a more specific matter than we might suppose that it is possible to know by such a means. The experiences are always intensely private; Wordsworth is alone, and the thing known is the relationship between his mind and that which is other than his mind. But "that which is other" is often, though vaguely described, undoubtedly God. In some cases, the atmosphere and associations of the place which gave rise to the knowing are Christian. And in the respect that all such knowings are self-knowings, Wordsworth sometimes knows himself to be an immortal creature, capable of knowing God. Some of the spots of time, then, are specifically religious, if not doctrinally explicit, and I shall need to examine some of these in detail. But first I want to look at one of the most personally specific of all these moments, wherein Wordsworth not merely knows what kind of creature he is, being man, but what kind of man he is, being a poet.

A principal characteristic of Wordsworth's notion of deliberate holiday is that it is often a kind of holiday on top of a holiday: the shepherd steals his pittance from strict time at the end of a sanctioned break from duty; Wordsworth, as we shall see in the Furness Abbey passage, and as we have already seen in the skating episode, achieves his visionary moment by taking holiday beyond that which he shares with his companions, beyond mechanical time, social time, and natural time, and even beyond the limits suggested by prudence. In *The Prelude*, 4:308–32, Wordsworth comes to his Godlike hour, his time of self-knowing and self-definition, by taking holiday from holiday itself.

> The memory of one particular hour
> Doth here rise up against me. 'Mid a throng
> Of maids and youths, old men, and matrons staid,

A medley of all tempers, I had passed
The night in dancing, gaiety, and mirth,
With din of instruments and shuffling feet,
And glancing forms, and tapers glittering,
And unaimed prattle flying up and down;
Spirits upon the stretch, and here and there
Slight shocks of young love-liking interspersed,
Whose transient pleasure mounted to the head,
And tingled through the veins. Ere we retired,
The cock had crowed, and now the eastern sky
Was kindling, not unseen, from humble copse
And open field, through which the pathway wound,
And homeward led my steps. Magnificent
The morning rose, in memorable pomp,
Glorious as e'er I had beheld—in front,
The sea lay laughing at a distance; near,
The solid mountains shone, bright as the clouds,
Grain-tinctured, drenched in empyrean light;
And in the meadows and the lower grounds
Was all the sweetness of a common dawn—
Dews, vapours, and the melody of birds,
And labourers going forth to till the fields.

There is no hint of self-reproach in the description of the dancing—the memory which rises up against him is not of the hours of merriment, but of the hour of vision on the mountain road, presumably because he feels that he has not fully met all the obligations of that hour. The lightness and rapid passing of pleasure is emphasized in the pace of the verse; the sense of superficially joyous experiences merely succeeding each other, not developing one from another, is reflected in the flat, chiming conjunctions:

dancing, gaiety and mirth,
With din of instruments and shuffling feet,
And glancing forms, and tapers glittering,
And unaimed prattle flying up and down;
Spirits upon the stretch, and here and there

The "ands" chime the night away. The first sign of a slackening of pace occurs when Wordsworth refers to "Slight shocks of young love-liking interspersed." The syllables stretch out as eyes and thoughts begin to linger on a particular object. The pleasure of such encounters may be transient, but it springs from an instinct that ultimately seeks stability. Significantly, it is after these delighted and appraising glances that the poetry begins to note the symbols of passing time. The crowing of the cock is one of those natural signals that human society has adopted for itself as the special emblem of both late reveling and early stirring. Indeed, it is because it is the symbol of both that it is so popular in this kind of context. To carouse through the night until the time when the ordinary man must leave his bed to go to work is the mark of a special kind of joy and freedom.

But of course, such a night represents only a rather special kind of relaxation. Unless we have made ourselves ill, the breaking up of such a party is another, and perhaps deeper, kind of relaxation. It is this sense of relief, this throwing down the social burden, that is really the deliberate holiday that is important in Wordsworth's lines. The verse acknowledges the effort and tension of social enjoyment both in its pace and in the rapid succession of images, as well as in the explicit statement "Spirits upon the stretch." Enjoying oneself and amusing one's companions can be a nerve-tightening business. The crowing of the cock is welcome, and it is the last shrill note in the night's music. From then on the passage deals with images of slowly growing splendor, relaxed sweetness, and a universal rejoicing in the undemanding commonplace.

When the sky kindles, another society is awakening as one society is going to rest. Moreover, the new society of morning is easy and unsophisticated, tied to its environmental time scheme and free from the tensions of independence. Wordsworth's homeward path winds through "humble copse / And open field." He goes to rest as nature rouses and laborers go forth to till the fields. That is his glory and his independence. But the special glory of this one particular hour resides in his throwing down the burden of that independence, in holiday from that privilege, in being utterly absorbed by the spectacle of a natural world so completely responsive to time that time does not exist. The hands of a clock do not know what time it is; only that which is other than a clock can read a clock. And Wordsworth has made himself other than a clock in two ways: first, and most obvious, while the spirit of the season prompts man to rouse and go forth, Wordsworth is on his way home to bed; second, for the society which he has just left, the great joy of the night is over, but for Wordsworth the flat social aftermath is the occasion of a supreme climax. He has moved outside both the social and natural time schemes. The occasion of the great experience, then, is both holiday and rest from holiday, a realization of independence and a relaxation from the burden of that independence. The glory that the poetry celebrates is the sweetness of a common dawn, seen not from the point of view of one responding to the spirit of the season, but by a privileged, deliberate idler from the vantage point of majestic indolence.

The nature of the experience one may define as the perception of a grand congruence of time patterns. The sun rises, and unsophisticated men and creatures rise with it—the glorious pomp and common sweetness are united in necessity. The creatures of necessity have their own splendor. All the "memorable pomp" seems to belong to and emanate from the rising sun, but it pertains equally to the natural, the necessitous, the unfree common beings: dews, vapors, birds, whatever stirs in copse and field, and laboring men so near to nature and its time that they scarcely know their independence. And in this harmony of man's time and nature's time, this union of grandeur and the commonplace, creation rejoices.

> The sea lay laughing at a distance; near,
> The solid mountains shone, bright as the clouds,
> Grain-tinctured, drenched in empyrean light.

All this is common. But Wordsworth is not common.

I have earlier referred to this Godlike hour as a self-defining hour; this is the hour, it is commonly agreed, when he knew himself to be a poet. It is to a poetic vocation he must be dedicated; to this use he must turn the power of his independence. Presumably critics agree on this interpretation because they feel he cannot be referring to anything else in lines 334–37.

> I made no vows, but vows
> Were then made for me; bond unknown to me
> Was given, that I should be, else sinning greatly,
> A dedicated Spirit.

But there is even more positive evidence in the passage. Wordsworth sees the night of gaiety and the common dawn together in a way only a great poet is likely to see them together. The poetry celebrates, among other things, this specifically poetic vision, the "observation of affinities / In objects where no brotherhood exists / To passive minds." Because of this experience, Wordsworth knows that his mind is not passive, for the passage is an example of his marvelous capacity to observe affinities. The throng in the gay room, the "medley of all tempers," becomes, out of doors, the stirring society of all manner of creatures in field and copse. The gaiety and mirth and prattle flying up and down are transmuted to the sea laughing at a distance; the din of instruments and shuffling feet modulates to the melody of birds; the brightness of the room, with tapers glittering, intensifies to "the solid mountains shone... drenched in empyrean light." The contrasts of the passage are direct and obvious, while the similarities emerge slowly, without assertion. As they do so they illustrate the truths that obsess the poetic imagination—that all figures are similes and that the most poetic simile of all is antithesis. A man is not a poet because he can record the similarity in things different; he is a poet because he can perceive it. This is what Wordsworth knows in his Godlike hour, and henceforth he can so define himself. But although critics speak of Wordsworth's Godlike hour, and although they recognize in terms such as "vows," "sinning greatly," and "dedicated spirit" specifically religious terminology, the experience itself is not religious. Wordsworth knows himself and his relationship to nature; he does not apprehend the divine. Other passages are more specifically religious, and to these I must now turn with all necessary caution.

The matter of Wordsworth's religious beliefs is such a potent cause of confusion and irritation and seems to present such an easy target for shallow-minded irony that the serious commentator may prefer to ignore it. In themselves, these beliefs have little relevance to most of Wordsworth's great poetry and indeed occupy little ground even in the authorized standard texts. However, some examination of them is unavoidable at this point, because the visionary moments I am about to examine were occasioned by visits to ruined Christian shrines, and Wordsworth's experiences clearly were affected by the fact that the ruins were Christian. My task is more difficult because there is no tradition of critical common sense on the matter. The commentators who address themselves to it seem determined to say something final and downright. Bernard Blackstone, for example, scorns Wordsworth's Christianity as a retreat from the Newtonian universe, which, he argues, the poet saw as "a remorseless continuum to be worshipped, feared, placated, and finally escaped from." On the other hand, writing at the end of the nineteenth century, William Hale White asserted: "Wordsworth worshipped the true God alone, from the days of *Lyrical Ballads* to his death, and set up no shrine to Baal."[6] That may be so, but if "the true God" is the God of Israel, the early great poetry usually suggests otherwise. In *The Recluse* Wordsworth boasts of passing unalarmed by Yahweh and his shouting angels; his encounters with God take place on the Clogwyn path, or on "the perilous ridge," hanging alone. God speaks to him with the voice of streams roaring from the cloud-covered Llanberis Pass, or in the "strange utterance" of "the loud dry wind"; immanent but not incarnate, he never looks like Jesus, and though Wordsworth certainly had a vivid consciousness of man's wickedness, little or nothing in his early work suggests that he had assimilated the notions of grace and redemption. He may appear to have done so in his later work, particularly where he is writing as a man explicitly committed to a denominational allegiance, but by the time he wrote *Ecclesiastical Sonnets* one may unkindly say that he had "normalized" his religious sentiments, and this process may well have been connected with his increasingly conservative political notions. To this extent, perhaps, his Anglicanism was "snug"—it was the right form of belief for any Englishman bothered about God, having nothing foreign about it except the Christian basis.

Hale White implies that despite all Wordsworth's gnosticism and animism, even in his early verse there is at least an embryonic Christian spirit. There is as much truth in this notion as in Blackstone's, but not more. Christianity is a learned religion, inevitably so since it is dogmatic and tied to historical events. The "motions of the viewless winds" may bring to the sensitive man powerful spiritual assurances, but they say nothing about what happened on Calvary. Natural religion of the kind Wordsworth seems to be expressing in certain passages of *The Prelude* can never be Christian according to the common implications of the word. We might, therefore, be able to agree with the simple view of Wordsworth as an apostate pagan if all the great mystical experiences were associated with lakes and crags, and if the intimations of divine presence were all huge and mighty forms pursuing the sinner or low breathings chastising him by fear. But what I now have to investigate are certain mystical experiences associated with the debris of ruined Catholic shrines, and in these cases specifically Christian allusions and sentiments are embedded in the poetry. (It is worth noting that this is as true of the 1805 version of *The Prelude* as of the 1850.) However, the Christian associations have a value not directly connected with the merits of Christianity itself, and this value is not dependent on belief in it. What happened to Wordsworth when he visited these shrines is akin, I think, to what happened to him crossing Westminster Bridge "on the roof / Of an itinerant vehicle": "A weight of ages did at once descend / Upon my heart."

It would be strange if, in examining at such length Wordsworth's consciousness of time, I totally ignored his sense of history. Byron, of course, is the Romantic poet who most immediately and fruitfully associates places and past events; in this respect there is no poem quite like *Childe Harold*. But if we think of Byron as typically the poet with a sense of history, we may well miss the value of Wordsworth's less spectacular historical consciousness. It is local and undramatic, manifesting itself in allusions rather than in specific and detailed imaginings. Indeed, Wordsworth's sense of history is a sense of tradition rather than events. Once having discerned the suggestions of tradition in the passages associated with the Christian shrines, we shall be able to identify a curious kind of vibration in the poetry—a shuttling between past and present time in our consciousness so rapid we are scarcely aware of it.

Herbert Lindenberger has drawn attention to a kind of resonance in all the spots of time passages. The reader, he says, is always aware of at least two points of time: the time at which he supposes Wordsworth to be writing and the time of the incident. The reader cannot therefore lose himself in the past, for he is always recalled to the "present" of the poem, the time of writing. The spot of time, therefore, is Wordsworth's characteristic method of probing the past. In one sense this method is a literary necessity. Wordsworth is telling a story, albeit a true one, and consequently the occasions of the moments of vision are always introduced casually, as if he were about to recount an anecdote merely. But the spots of time are more subtly organized than mere anecdotes would be, for the past becomes a means of setting emotion at a manageable distance. At the same time, the interaction of past and present sets free long-forgotten feel-

ings, giving new life and energy to the present. As Lindenberger says, "The energies latent in Wordsworth's memories
are like rays of light that pass through a prism and reveal
constantly new possibilities of colour to the observing eye."[7]
But in the passages I am about to examine the interaction is more complex than this, for one must take into account a more remote past than the past represented by the
moment of experience. The reader's mind therefore not only
works back and forth between the time of writing and the
time of the incident, but between both of these and the past
which was perceived at the time of the incident and which
was a necessary part of the experience. The usual reverberations start more distant echoes and are counterpointed by
them; one's time sense is no longer a matter of *now* and *then*,
for both *now* and *then* are burdened by "a weight of ages."*

Let us now look at the Chapel Island passage (*Prelude*,
10:511–28), which deals with the death of Robespierre, leader
of the Jacobin group under whose regime the Reign of Terror
was instituted.

> O Friend! few happier moments have been mine
> Than that which told the downfall of this Tribe
> So dreaded, so abhorred. The day deserves
> A separate record. Over the smooth sands
> Of Leven's ample estuary lay
> My journey, and beneath a genial sun,
> With distant prospect among gleams of sky
> And clouds, and intermingling mountain-tops,
> In one inseparable glory clad,
> Creatures of one ethereal substance met
> In consistory, like a diadem
> Or crown of burning seraphs as they sit

---

*It is obviously a help to the reader to have some knowledge of the shrines which
Wordsworth is describing, since we can fairly safely assume that the poet himself
had such knowledge. The history of these shrines is, however, not easily available to
the general reader, being found largely in books locally published in limited editions
and now available only in small public libraries in the Lake District of England. I
have therefore included a brief historical sketch of each of these shrines in the
Appendix.

> In the empyrean. Underneath that pomp
> Celestial, lay unseen the pastoral vales
> Among whose happy fields I had grown up
> From childhood. On the fulgent spectacle,
> That neither passed away nor changed, I gazed
> Enrapt.

That in a general way this "fulgent spectacle" resembles a vision of heaven or of a kind of congress of angels is obvious enough. But the resemblance is presented as something more than a mere likeness; it is not a chance arrangement of water vapor. It is a manifestation of heaven's ultimate authority, and the symbolism is reinforced by a familiar Wordsworthian syntactical device of suggesting a construction that is never completed. "Distant prospect" leads one to expect an "of" followed by a noun, and the preposition "among" seems merely to introduce a qualifying adjunct. Somewhere "among" the clouds that are being described is the thing or things of which we seem to have been promised a prospect. The "of" never comes, for the "of" in "of one ethereal substance" plainly must be construed with "Creatures," not "prospect." Yet because there is an "of," the mind tends to grasp it and make it replace the "of" that seems to have been lost. Thus we seem to see among the clouds "Creatures of one ethereal substance met / In consistory... a crown of burning seraphs." A second reading, of course, restores the true syntax: "Creatures," "diadem," and "crown of burning seraphs" are all in apposition to "sky," "clouds," and "mountain tops." But meanwhile, the visionary suggestion has been made, and it is kept active by terms such as "empyrean" and "pomp / Celestial" and by the clear scriptural echoes of "neither passed away nor changed."

But this moment of rapture is not the supremely happy moment referred to in the first line of the passage, though clearly it contributes to and is a premonition of it. Wordsworth has not yet heard of Robespierre's death, though he will do so shortly. He spends a few moments meditating another death, that of his old schoolmaster, whose grave he had visited that morning. According to the 1805 version of *The Prelude,* the grave was'in "Cartmell's rural Town" (10:533), where there was another ruined shrine, something of whose history Wordsworth must certainly have known, and whose condition at that time was rather dramatically symbolic of the capacity of a religious tradition to survive hostile attack and physical destruction. The splendid vision above the Leven sands, seeming to show a kind of heavenly council presiding above earthly affairs, perhaps turned Wordsworth's thoughts towards Cartmel again. In the context of the entire Chapel Island passage, the visit to the grave serves as a contrast to the death of Robespierre: a poet seeks out the grave of the good, unknown schoolteacher and weeps there; crowds cheer and rejoice at the death of the evil public man. The gods are just, and Wordsworth has seen the heavenly powers "in consistory" like "burning seraphs."

The description of the moment of hearing the great news maintains the religious tone and alludes to Chapel Island's tradition of prayer. Wordsworth approached the shrine, where once "the vested priest / Said matins" (ll. 559–60), by the so-called Way of the Sands. At that time these sands still provided the only direct route from Lancaster to the Cartmel and Furness peninsulas. From Lancaster the route lay across the sands at Hest Bank as far as the course of the River Kent, where it was necessary for travellers to look carefully for the day's best fording place, which changed perpetually owing to varying currents. This difficulty overcome, the route continued across the sands to Kent's Bank on the Cartmel Peninsula.[8] Here, on solid ground again, travellers no doubt felt a temporary relief, for the route they had taken was extremely dangerous. The sands were covered by the tide twice in twenty-four hours, and the place where they had stopped to "prospect" for the ford might at high tide be covered by twelve feet of water.

But the Cartmel Peninsula was merely a stepping stone between two wide and dangerous fords. At Sandgate on the western shore, the Way of the Sands began its most perilous course across the four miles of the Leven estuary, and part of the way along this route was situated the "small / And rocky island" (ll. 554–55) on which, in 1325, the abbot of Furness had established a chapel where monks prayed continually for the welfare of voyagers.[9] When Wordsworth made his crossing, all that remained of the chapel was "a dilapidated structure" (l. 558) encrusted with shells and seaweed. But the Way of the Sands, in spite of its dangers, was still the preferred route to and from Furness Peninsula.

> Not far from that still ruin all the plain
> Lay spotted with a variegated crowd
> Of vehicles and travellers, horse and foot,
> Wading beneath the conduct of their guide
> In loose procession through the shallow stream
> Of inland waters.
>
>   (Ll. 562–66)

As Wordsworth advances upon this scene of "gentleness and peace" (l. 554), the leader of the "loose procession" hails him with the words "Robespierre is dead!" Wordsworth's response is plainly and devoutly religious.

> Great was my transport, deep my gratitude
> To everlasting Justice, by this fiat
> Made manifest. 'Come now, ye golden times,'
> Said I forth-pouring on those open sands
> A hymn of triumph: 'as the morning comes
> From out the bosom of the night, come ye:
> Thus far our trust is verified; behold!
> They who with clumsy desperation brought
> A river of Blood, and preached that nothing else
> Would cleanse the Augean stable, by the might
> Of their own helper have been swept away;
> Their madness stands declared and visible;
> Elsewhere will safety now be sought, and earth
> March firmly towards righteousness and peace,'—
> Then schemes I framed more calmly, when and how

> The madding factions might be tranquillised,
> And how through hardships manifold and long
> The glorious renovation would proceed.
>
> (Ll. 576–93)

The crowd now gathered in the vicinity of the "Romish chapel" are sight-seeing tourists, but the presence of this multitude may remind the reader that travellers used to rest there, hear mass, and offer thanks that their greatest dangers were past.

The excitement of the crowd is not so closely defined; one may suppose it to have been largely unreflecting jubilation, perhaps not even connected with the thought that a dictatorship had fallen, but simply demonstrating the chauvinistic joy of seeing major troubles in the enemy camp. But Wordsworth's jubilation is that of a Girondist, not an English Tory. The revolution can now proceed without terror and violence; the "glorious renovation" will be achieved by hardship and toil. Wordsworth reveals more than loyalty to a particular revolutionary faction, however. The Jacobins were overthrown by "the might of their own helper"—the Terror which they themselves established had defeated them. It is a pattern of retribution which suggests the divine irony by which God sometimes seems to assert his justice. Hence Wordsworth's gratitude is poured out, not to the opportunist group in the French National Convention who engineered the Jacobin downfall, but to "everlasting Justice, by this fiat / Made manifest."

Many people will, with some reason, suspect that the religious sentiments Wordsworth expresses in these lines belong to the time of writing rather than to the time of the experience. (They are not 1850 revisions, for a glance at de Selincourt's parallel texts shows only one change in the religious expressions. The "everlasting Justice" of 1850 was merely "eternal justice" in 1805.)[10] There is, after all, evidence of his youthful cavalier humanism brushing aside Yahweh and his angels in *The Recluse*. But it is possible that

the events of the Chartreuse really caused a certain faltering in
this attitude. A man may feel religion to be irrelevant or a
hindrance to necessary social action and yet be alarmed when
he sees it under determined attack. What will the world be
like, he may ask with some misgivings, when religion has
altogether disappeared? Therefore, when the military came to
turn the nuns out of the convent at Chartreuse, Wordsworth
seemed to hear the voice of nature herself protesting: "Stay,
stay your sacrilegious hands" (*Prelude*, 6:430). I should note,
by the way, that although the protesting passage from which
this line is taken did not appear in the 1805 version, a long
passage of similar tone and sentiment was inserted in an early
revision, the so-called A2 manuscript. [11]

Certainly both the 1805 and the 1850 versions indicate
that Wordsworth's objections to Robespierre included religious matters. While visiting the town of Arras he had reflected that it was the birthplace of the man who afterwards
"Wielded the sceptre of the Atheist crew" (1850, 10:502;
1805, 10:458). And now religious faith is vindicated in the
poetic justice of Robespierre's death. Wordsworth's cry of
gratitude to "everlasting Justice by this fiat / Made manifest"
is like Albany's on hearing of his brother-in-law Cornwall's
death in act 4 of *King Lear:*

> This shows you are above,
> You justicers, that these our nether crimes
> So speedily can venge.

And Wordsworth, a few minutes before hearing the news,
has been enrapt by a vision of the "justicers," the "Creatures
of one ethereal substance met. . . . " The revolutionary militia
may turn the unworldly votaries out of the Chartreuse, yet
still the cross of Jesus stands erect as if hands of angelic powers had planted it there; Cromwell may batter down the
Romish chapel on Leven sands, but it is built on a "rocky
island . . . / Itself like a sea rock." Though it has been hundreds of years since the vested priest said matins for the faith-

ful, the people are at the chapel again, crowding around the seaweed-strewn and shell-encrusted shrine at the very moment when God's eternal fiat is made manifest in the condign fate of "the Atheist crew." Until the ninth of Thermidor (July 27, 1794), when Robespierre's enemies achieved their coup d'etat, the Jacobins in the National Convention seemingly had in their hands all the physical means of power, but it is in the consistory of burning seraphs that the ultimate power resides, and this has now been made apparent. The death of Robespierre, then, is for Wordsworth a cause for religious thanksgiving for a great deliverance, and thanksgiving of this kind had for centuries been offered by travellers who had risked their lives crossing the Way of the Sands. The poet's prayer renews an old tradition.

Wordsworth himself had traveled along those sands many times in his childhood, and perhaps the religious tone of the experience he describes in the passage I have just discussed gains something from the memory, referred to in lines 595–603, of a state of mystical rapture which he experienced during one of his schoolboy visits to Furness Abbey, and which he has described more fully in *The Prelude*, 2:102–28. Before one can deal adequately with these lines, however, it is necessary to look very carefully at a passage concerned with another ruined shrine, situated on the island of Lady Holme in Windermere. Beautiful in itself, the passage prepares the reader's sensibility for the Furness Abbey lines which follow a little later.

> When summer came,
> Our pastime was, on bright half-holidays,
> To sweep along the plain of Windermere
> With rival oars; and the selected bourne
> Was now an Island musical with birds
> That sang and ceased not; now a Sister Isle
> Beneath the oaks' umbrageous covert, sown
> With lilies of the valley like a field;
> And now a third small Island, where survived
> In solitude the ruins of a shrine

> Once to Our Lady dedicate, and served
> Daily with chaunted rites.
>
> (*Prelude*, 2:54–65)

In lines 65–93, we are given some little time to listen to Wordsworth lecturing on vainglory and modesty and reminiscing about his spartan schoolboy lodgings. It is rather dull stuff, but it is a strategic dullness during which the reader begins to forget the precise imagery associated with Lady Holme. When very similar images recur in the Furness Abbey passage, they seem like teasing memories of the sort that create a happy dislocation of one's sense of time.

The suggestion that time is not quite behaving in its normal straight-line sequence occurs first in the Lady Holme lines themselves, with a deliberate echo of Caliban's description of Ariel's music in act 3 of *The Tempest*.

> Be not afeard, the isle is full of noises
> Sounds and sweet airs, that give delight and hurt not.
>
> an Island musical with birds
> That sang and ceased not.

Asking ourselves, "Where I have I heard that before?" is a most potent stimulation of the exploration of time past. And when we have tracked the memory down, the allusion supplies an airy sprite, agent of a benevolent spiritual power; the island is magical, set apart from the temporal mainland. The impression is strengthened by ambiguity. If Wordsworth had added a final "d" to "dedicate," then "served" would have been obviously a parallel construction: "Once . . . dedicated; once served daily." However, a first reading construes it with "survived": "A shrine once dedicated to Our Lady still survived at this time, and was still served daily with chaunted rites." But this interpretation produces the wrong meaning in a literal sense. The reader is therefore predisposed to accept a metaphorical meaning, and his attention immediately lights on the birds "that sang and ceased not." These birds already bring with them suggestions of Ariel's music. But while they satisfy his need for metaphorical interpretation, they distract him from noticing that they are on the wrong island. Wordsworth has thus partially dislocated the normal consciousness of time and space.

He does so for two reasons: first, to suggest the persistence or resurrection of the tradition of prayer on Lady Holme; and second, to enrich the Furness Abbey passage by smuggling these suggestions into the later lines as a species of déjà vu experience. For in lines 65–93, he allows these shifting and merging impressions to sink from the immediate surface of the reader's attention. The intervening verse has a deliberately ordinary tone and deals with commonplace moral abstractions. In the Furness Abbey lines, all of the suggestions of Prospero's Windermere island will be deftly manipulated in the reader's memory, producing the sense of a remembered reality of which the present reality of the abbey nave seems an echo or a repetition. And this in turn suggests that it is the remoter past of the abbey that is reverberating in his mind, a tradition that is felt to persist among the ruins.

My examination of the Furness Abbey lines must necessarily be long and complicated, not because I am trying to identify an ineffable experience, but because this passage is great poetry. Properly to evaluate the passage, to track down all its subtleties and nuances, demands an unusual degree of cross-reference, and one must be more than usually prepared to find precision in apparent ambiguity. The passage deals with the strenuous leisure of Wordsworth's schooldays. He and his friends hire horses during their free time and gallop away to visit some religious ruin, Christian or pagan, either an old fane where once the druids worshipped or

> the antique walls
> Of that large abbey, where within the Vale
> Of Nightshade, to St Mary's honour built,
> Stands yet a mouldering pile with fractured arch,

Belfry, and images, and living trees,
A holy scene! Along the smooth green turf
Our horses grazed. To more than inland peace
Left by the west wind sweeping overhead
From a tumultuous ocean, trees and towers
In that sequestered valley may be seen,
Both silent and both motionless alike;
Such the deep shelter that is there, and such
The safeguard for repose and quietness.
  Our steeds remounted and the summons given,
With whip and spur we through the chauntry flew
In uncouth race, and left the cross-legged knight,
And the stone-abbot, and that single wren
Which one day sang so sweetly in the nave
Of the old church, that—though from recent showers
The earth was comfortless, and touched by faint
Internal breezes, sobbings of the place
And respirations, from the roofless walls
The shuddering ivy dripped large drops—yet still
So sweetly 'mid the gloom the invisible bird
Sang to herself, that there I could have made
My dwelling-place, and lived for ever there
To hear such music.

                                    (*Prelude*, 2:102–28)

The reader's memory is immediately alerted by "to St Mary's
honour built," an obvious link with "Once to Our Lady
dedicate." The connection is mildly disturbing because the
difference between Furness Abbey and the Lady Holme
shrine has been plainly indicated. The latter consisted of a few
stones and a cave on an island, but the Furness Abbey ruins
are massive. However, the reader is immediately distracted
from this fact by the poet's ingenious disturbance of his ordinary habits of recognizing passing time. Present participles
suggest continuous action, so that the phrase "mouldering
pile with fractured arch" encourages us to see the process of
crumbling going on. But "living trees" suggests a truly visible motion and thus by contrast freezes the image of collapse
at the very moment we had begun to picture it.

Wordsworth has engineered a dilemma in our imaginative and associative thinking. For the moment we cannot decide which is the symbol of endurance, the motionless but decaying ruin or the living, and therefore moving, trees. To some people this ambiguity is a weakness in the poetry; it is a typical Wordsworthian trick to evoke vague sensations and subdue the intellectual energy of the reader. But Wordsworth is in fact stimulating the mind to very rapid activity indeed, and the interpretative dilemma reflects a philosophical dilemma. What endures? Nature (the living trees)? Or the mind of man (the abbey as an expression of his spiritual hungers)? Or nothing? The living trees will one day fall, and the abbey is ruined and mouldering. But apart from this kind of uncertainty, Wordsworth uses the symbols of stillness and movement most carefully to promote an impression that something odd is happening to our sense of time, and while we are still trying to formulate and identify our impressions, he pronounces confidently and unambiguously, "A holy scene!" And the holiness, the timelessness, is reinforced by contrast, for our glance is now directed to the horses, neither timeless nor holy, but merely grazing.

The suggestion of a scene exempt from time is strengthened in the emphasis on the secluded location of the valley. The wind from a tumultuous ocean sweeps "overhead"—tumult and motion, the visual attributes of time, pass over the valley. In lines 110–12 we look again at the mouldering pile and find that our bewildered time sense has been reoriented, for both stones and trees are still: "Both silent and both motionless alike." We are sequestered from time; the valley is a safeguard for repose and is blessed with more than inland peace. The calm suggested is the calm of the weight of ages, for the phrases set off long historical echoes. The abbey had for centuries enjoyed a special kind of repose and peace, being sequestered from the world of time and change in a very literal sense.

In lines 115–17, contrast is necessary once more. Wordsworth and his companions leap onto their horses and gallop noisily away. Their sudden muscular energy reminds us that they are finite and alive, for during the previous lines the boys have remained in the hinterland of our minds as figures entranced and still, or perhaps prone, like the effigies on the tombs. And when the boys come precipitately to life, we notice for the first time the real effigies, the "cross-legged knight / And the stone-abbot." The effect is parallel to that created by the juxtaposition of "mouldering pile" and "living trees," and our grasp of reality and permanence is again bewildered. Although the effigies are as immediately present as the boys, they represent a reality belonging to the remote past. We must assume a time when knights and abbots moved about the abbey as lively as the boys. Two kinds of contrast strike us at once: the contrast of the living boys with the stone figures and the contrast of those figures with the living reality of the past which they represent. And it is in these contrasts of life and death, past and present, that we sense vibration in the poetry, as our attention shuttles rapidly between several points of time.

Before the effect of these antitheses can subside, Wordsworth engages us in a long periodic sentence in which he carefully refrains from describing the wren's song, except to say that it was sweet. The manner in which this sentence operates needs close attention. The casual phrase "one day" does not necessarily mean the same day as the one so far described. But is any particular occasion being described? The whole passage is introduced with reference to habitual visits to such places (ll. 95–103). The poet first pictures the abbey, one supposes, from memories of several visits. The ruin, not the occasion, is being described. But suddenly, with a single detail, the vision focuses on a particular scene noted on a particular visit: "along the smooth green turf / Our horses grazed." Out of the shifting composite of memories, a single picture has separated itself. But this is not necessarily the same occasion as the supreme experience of the wren's song. The time shift is as casual as the shift from general to particular. This is how emotion is recollected in tran-

quility—from the generalized store of softly contoured images, a few precise and vivid impressions present themselves
with clear outlines. And perhaps this is true of the visionary
moment—it can only be known as such after it has happened.
Out of many similar days, the moment of knowing has been
experienced "one day," and the phrase economically conveys
the random, unprocurable nature of such experience. But the
phrase is also unobtrusive enough to allow both occasions,
the day the wren sang so sweetly and the day the horses
grazed, to coalesce, the images of one contributing to the
total effect of the other.

All the careful preparation of the previous lines is now
fully exploited. As soon as the wren is mentioned, our
memories transfer to the ruined abbey the already mingled
imagery of the Windermere islands: the shrine "Once to Our
Lady dedicate," still "served daily with chaunted rites," the
chaunts being those of the birds that "sang and ceased not."
The effect thus produced is akin to that of delayed cognition,
which is often taken for a kind of clairvoyant recognition of
something that is happening for the first time. But in these
lines the total effect of the sense of reminiscence is more
complicated than the common experience. The ambiguity of
"served / Daily with chaunted rites" in the Lady Holme passage now modifies our response to the words before us in a
delicate and cunning manner. The song of the wren recalls
the birds which, by misconstruction of the syntax, we
momentarily transferred from the island "musical with
birds" to the Lady Holme shrine, which in turn by misconstruction of the syntax we supposed to be still "served /
Daily with chaunted rites." The nave of the old church thus
blends with the shrine "Once to Our Lady dedicate," and the
wren's song is a daily chaunted rite. The birds on the Windermere island "sang and ceased not"; the wren, it seems,
will cease not. The bird that chaunts "mid the gloom" of the
nave, like the light-winged dryad of the trees, was not born
for death. The bird seems both real and symbolic, possibly a
spiritual agent (the singing of the birds on Windermere recalls

Ariel's music) continuing in the ruins the devotions which
priest and choir can no longer perform. By suggesting this,
of course, the bird reminds us again of the pre-Reformation
past of the abbey and sets off more reverberations apart from
those touched off by the memories of Lady Holme. Possibly
too the bird symbolizes the indestructibility of a tradition, as
could quite literally be seen at Cartmel.

The total effect, however, is richer than mere symbolism. To strengthen the feelings "analogous to the supernatural," in lines 121–24 Wordsworth introduces a characteristically animist kind of imagery in "Internal breezes, sobbings of the place / and respirations." The lines imply the
kind of presence which is expressed more explicitly in "Nutting": "with gentle hand / Touch, for there is a spirit in the
woods." The suggestion of a spirit in the shrine finds a manifestation easily enough in the singing wren, but this is a first
impression only, for the spirit of the place is a spirit in travail
and sorrow: "sobbings of the place" connects with "shuddering ivy" and "large drops." All of these phrases suggest a
genius of the place mourning for the present ruin. The
sweetness of the bird's song is a contrast: the earth is comfortless, but the bird seems to be a comforter, offering an enrap-
turing sweetness "mid the gloom" and having about it
hints of spiritual endurance. The bird therefore begins to
gather to itself suggestions of the Holy Spirit, suggestions
strengthened by the word "invisible" and the clear invoca-
tion of the Christian tradition with the memory of Psalm 23:
"there I could have made / My dwelling place, and lived for
ever there" ("I will dwell in the House of the Lord forever").

Finally, there is a symbol of passing time that the reader
almost overlooks: "So sweetly mid the gloom the invisible
bird / Sang to herself." The "gloom" may simply be some
dark corner of the ruined nave, but there remains the suggestion of dusk. On this occasion at least, Wordsworth seems to
have stayed irresponsibly late in view of the long return journey (the Robespierre lines, in which Wordsworth remembers
the visit or visits in question, speak of riding home "Along

the margin of the moonlight sea"), and to have remained motionless as the knight and the stone abbot, entranced and unaware of failing daylight's commonsense message. "Gloom" therefore indicates a state of prolonged enchantment, with all the body's physiological clocks running slow and "even the motion of our human blood / Almost suspended."

In all this analysis I have been noting ambiguities, cross-references that seem to promote confusion, a coalescing of time, place, and imagery meant, I think, to produce vague sensations of the numinous, nebulous feelings of spiritual presence. Yet all of these things are the sources of strength in the poetry; all of the ambiguity is a necessary means of stating something precisely. The statement cannot be reproduced exactly except by copying out the poetry once more; all the critic can do is to try to indicate the nature of the experience being described and Wordsworth's possible state of mind at the time he described it.

The experience was real. Wordsworth may often have tinkered with the memories of his youthful experiences, but there is no reason to suppose that he simply fabricates anything. And the experience does seem to have been mystical in the traditional sense. For example, the boys came to the Lady Holme and the Furness Abbey ruins by rowing or riding, means involving great muscular effort. Furthermore, both activities involve strict physical control, bodily equilibrium, and nervous and physiological alertness of a high order. Disaster can come in an instant if the mental tension is relaxed. Yet when the boys reach the ruins, they can throw off the burden of taking care of themselves, relax utterly, and merely absorb what the environment has to offer. William James has something pertinent to say about this situation.

> The transition from tenseness, self-responsibility, and worry, to equanimity, receptivity, and peace, is the most wonderful of all those shiftings of inner equilibrium, those changes of the personal centre of energy, which I have

analyzed so often; and the chief wonder of it is that it so often comes about, not by doing, but by simply relaxing and throwing the burden down. This abandonment of self-responsibility seems to be the fundamental act in specifically religious, as distinguished from moral practice. It antedates theologies and is independent of all philosophies.[12]

We have returned to the notion of deliberate holiday in its most sublime and radical form. It seems likely that this particular kind of holiday is only possible to those who already have religious faith; the "abandonment of self-responsibility" may be possible only if one is already certain that there is a God who will take up what has been thus flung down, or whose constant providence is in this outright manner being acknowledged. That being so, the sense that God has taken up the burden may well be a self-deception supplied by the already held faith, and part of that faith's psychological function. Whatever it is, this is the experience Wordsworth describes in this passage. Let us look at the implications of "there I could have made / My dwelling place." For Wordsworth, far from Hawkshead, far from his revered schoolmaster and his frugal dame, with darkness coming down and a long ride to come, the damp and windy ruin has become home. Why should he wish to live forever there? To hear such music? This is hyperbole surely, a way of saying how delightful the wren's singing was. But the whole passage suggests something far more important. The sense of self-abandonment in lines 126–28 is so strong that a sense of being possessed seems a necessary complement to it. He abandons himself because he now feels that he is in another's care, the other represented by the bird and its singing. He is physically in God's house, though that structure is ruined; nevertheless, it is perhaps this sense of being "in the House of the Lord" and the sense of the permanence of spiritual tradition which the whole experience has promoted, that prompts the echo of the twenty-third psalm.

At this stage in his life Wordsworth was orphaned, and his home was not his father's house but Anne Tyson's cottage. One can imagine the kind of emotional needs this experience satisfied, and many people will be inclined to think that those very needs in some way produced the experience. Nevertheless, it was the kind of experience that William James identifies as specifically and exclusively religious.

> There is a state of mind, known to religious men, but to no others, in which the will to assert ourselves and hold our own has been displaced by a willingness to close our mouths and be as nothing in the floods and waterspouts of God. In this state of mind, what we most dreaded has become the habitation of our safety, and the hour of our moral death has turned into our spiritual birthday. The time for tension in our soul is over, and that of happy relaxation, of calm deep breathing, of an eternal present, with no discordant future to be anxious about, has arrived. Fear is not held in abeyance as it is by mere morality, it is positively expunged and washed away.[13]

> Although the oncoming of mystical states may be facilitated by preliminary voluntary operations, as by fixing the attention, or going through certain bodily performances, or in other ways which manuals of mysticism prescribe; yet when the characteristic sort of consciousness once has set in, the mystic feels as if his own will were in abeyance, and indeed sometimes as if he were grasped and held by a superior power.[14]

The whole Furness Abbey experience fits so well with James's descriptions that its authenticity can scarcely be doubted. Wordsworth is not fabricating. Nevertheless, knowing Wordsworth's tinkering habits, some commentators would be strongly inclined to suggest that the experience has been "normalized" by the time it reaches the page and that a natural animist response is merely being vested in Christian garments. The first shrine mentioned is druidic, and the evocation of the Holy Spirit in the wren's song is powerfully counterbalanced by lines 121–24.

But the animist and orthodox implications do not conflict. The wren's song blends naturally with the "internal

breezes" and "sobbings," the genius which these phrases
suggest is the spirit of a Christian hallowed place, and the
druidic ivy grows on the walls of a Cistercian ruin. Moreover, Wordsworth's "eternal present" may be shaped, not by
piety, but by a sense of Christian history. If the poet under-
took any revising of sentiment in this passage, it shows itself
not as a simple mixture or grafting on, but as a perfectly
natural coalescence. But there is really no ground for suppos-
ing any such revision; the moment of knowing, the "eternal
present," grew naturally out of the place, the self-abandonment, and the weight of ages.

7

The Source of Time

Only a naive or perverse reader would suppose that when Wordsworth wrote "there I could have
made / My dwelling-place, and lived for ever there / To hear
such music" (*Prelude,* 2:126–28), he meant "there" to refer
merely to the ruined nave of Furness Abbey and "such
music" to refer simply to the wren's song. Rather, the adverb
of place also designates a privileged state of consciousness,
and the music is the substance of what is experienced during
such consciousness. It is the state described by William James
in the extracts quoted at the end of chapter 6: "a willingness
to close our mouths and be as nothing," "happy relaxation,"
"calm deep breathing," and "fear is expunged and washed
away." What is experienced is an "eternal present." Now,
we could see such a state of consciousness, if we liked, as a
triumphantly successful piece of self-hypnosis and a symptom of a kind of mental illness. But we do not in fact have to
suppose a morbid condition in the poet in order to see what
kind of fear is expunged by the mystical rapture, for it is a

normal human fear. Matthew in "The Fountain" envies the blackbird and the lark their inability to wage a foolish strife with nature; Burns envies his mouse for being touched only by present disaster. Men can remember what has been and surmise what will be, but this more often than not means that they lament the past and fear the future. One need not postulate an orphan feeling betrayed by his dead mother or a young man tortured by incestuous pangs in order to see that Wordsworth's mysticism fulfills a need. It is a common need, arising from the very business of "the mind encountering its world." If the lamented past and the dreaded future can be gathered into an eternal present and calmly seen as parts of a benevolent and harmonious unity of all things, then we have achieved an invulnerable security. The need is plain, and the satisfaction of it is plain. Moreover, no one need be censorious about either the need or the form of the satisfaction, particularly when, as in Wordsworth's case, the mysticism seems to have done no harm and can be shown to have produced great poetry.

Let me now try to be a little less vague about Wordsworth's "eternal present." (Although James uses the phrase to describe all mystical visionary moments, it can be fittingly appropriated to Wordsworth's "spots of time.") With remarkable consistency, Wordsworth achieves his visionary state by stepping westward, so to speak, against the motion of the great clock, or by moving outside the clock, so that he sees time working, the earth rolling with visible motion her diurnal round. His moment is timeless then, or outside time, belonging to what medieval theologians would have called the permanence of God. Assuming as I must for present purposes that expressions such as "timelessness," "eternal present," and "the permanence of God" do all have one real meaning, then the problem for the poet is how to express that reality, to say what it is like in such a state or how things look viewed from there. Wordsworth's poetic career was not merely a quest for permanence, but a quest for the expression of permanence, and his failures are sublime. With the good sense that people find so surprising in mystics, he realized early that the matter could only be expressed obliquely, and that he must keep his readers in the company of flesh and blood and rocks and stones and trees. Hence his determination to use the tangible world in order to arouse a sense of something transcendent. He looked always for something in common experience, some natural object or phenomenon, which suggested the thing that could not be said directly. He certainly found natural objects which seem to be tokens of immortality—the River Duddon and Matthew's streamlet, for example. And anyone can see the vegetation cycle as a pulse which suggests an inexhaustible energy in nature, providing, that is, that he has never heard of entropy. Rossetti's Blessed Damozel, leaning vertiginously over heaven's expensive handrail, sees "Time like a pulse shake fierce / Through all the worlds." Wordsworth's Pedlar imagines a slower pulse.

> in the after-day
> Of boyhood, many an hour in caves forlorn,
> And 'mid the hollow depths of naked crags
> He sate, and even in their fixed lineaments,
> Or from the power of a peculiar eye,
> Or by creative feeling overborne,
> Or by predominance of thought oppressed,
> Even in their fixed and steady lineaments
> He traced an ebbing and a flowing mind,
> Expression ever varying!
>
> (*Excursion*, 1:153–62)

The "fixed lineaments" may imply to the youthful Pedlar an ebbing and flowing mind of God, but for the modern reader it is the landscape itself that ebbs and flows, in imaginatively accelerated physical change. One effect of this vision of geological time is to suggest by force of contrast the brevity of human life. A second effect is to suggest that there is in nature a perpetually creative and recreative energy: the universe is not running down; the Pedlar conceives of the pulsa-

tion of God's creative action while his eye is fixed on those
"steady lineaments." The Pedlar's vision may seem to point
forward to the astrophysicists' steady state theory of the universe, but whereas the Pedlar would see God as the source of
perpetual creation, Professor Fred Hoyle almost certainly
would not. And the steady state theory itself suggests, like
the pulsation concept, nothing more than unending time.

But the natural world presents something more like an
eternal present if we can see in one glance a whole cycle of
change and renewal, as Wordsworth could during his journey across the Alps with Jones.

> A march it was of military speed,
> And Earth did change her images and forms
> Before us, fast as clouds are changed in heaven.
>
> *(Prelude, 6:491–93)*

This journey had something of the nature of time-travelling;
Wordsworth and Jones dropped from winter through spring
into summer, and climbed into winter again on the next
ridge. And at the end of the Rhone glacier the extreme seasons were present together.

> There doth the reaper bind the yellow sheaf,
> The maiden spread the haycock in the sun,
> While Winter like a well-tamed lion walks,
> Descending from the mountain to make sport
> Among the cottages by beds of flowers.
>
> (Ll. 536–40)

The glacier itself is an image of time standing still, a fixed
mass in a posture of movement: "A motionless array of
mighty waves." But these images are merely premonitory
hints; the major experience took place in the Simplon Pass.

In the passage which describes the Simplon Pass experience (*Prelude*, 6:621–40), Wordsworth makes no pretense of
developing a logical argument. Impressions follow impressions, becoming less precise and more portentous as the pas-

sage goes on. The total effect seems to be of an indefinable religious experience, though medical materialism would perhaps sabotage this impression by pointing to evidence of Wordsworth's unaccustomed vertigo in "the sick sight / And giddy prospect" (ll. 632–33). Certain fundamental religious notions are suggested: for example, the union of opposites in phrases such as "Tumult and peace, the darkness and the light" (l. 635). "First and last" (l. 640) in this context may well remind the reader of the alpha and omega of *Revelation*. There are Thomistic arguments, perhaps, implicit in "workings of one mind" (l. 636). But there are really only two images which are specifically symbols of the eternal present, and they are seen almost in the same instant.

> The immeasurable height
> Of woods decaying, never to be decayed,
> The stationary blasts of waterfalls.
>
> (Ll. 624–26)

"Woods decaying, never to be decayed" (l. 625) suggests that they cover so great a range on the mountainsides that it is possible to see a whole seasonal cycle, even a whole life cycle, in a single glance. To add force to the point, this image is immediately followed by that of the waterfalls, another image of time standing still. It is more subtle than the glacier image, since these waters are in roaring motion. Finally Wordsworth states the matter explicitly.

> Characters of the great Apocalypse,
> The types and symbols of Eternity,
> Of first, and last, and midst, and without end.
>
> (Ll. 638–40)

In looking for symbols of eternity in the visible world, we would not expect to find anything very satisfactory in the things man has made, even among those productions which we are in the habit of calling immortal. Wordsworth laments in *The Prelude,* 5:19–165 that the fruits of the human mind can find no medium which is proof against ultimate physical destruction. If the consecrated works of bard and sage cannot survive a second flood, much less then should we expect to find intimations of immortality in the material things man has built. Objects made to symbolize religious ideas seem to be all we can really point to: a crucifix or a mandala, a church, temple, or synagogue. Wordsworth takes due note of these. While in France, exulting in the liberating violence of the Revolution, he is disturbed by the sight of troops with "arms flashing, and a military glare!" They are evidently on their way to turn the nuns out of the Chartreuse.

> —'Stay, stay your sacrilegious hands!'—The voice
> Was Nature's, uttered from her Alpine throne;
> I heard it then and seem to hear it now—
> 'Your impious work forbear, perish what may,
> Let this one temple last, be this one spot
> Of earth devoted to eternity!'
>
> (*Prelude,* 6:430–35)

Whether or not Wordsworth deduced nature's prohibition from a thunderclap or a sudden roar of wind, it seems that he is not merely using a rhetorical device. The idea is not, for him, a spontaneous act of his own mind, but an utterance from outside himself, to which he replies:

> 'be the house redeemed
> With its unworldly votaries, for the sake
> Of conquest over sense, hourly achieved
> Through faith and meditative reason, resting
> Upon the word of heaven-imparted truth,
> Calmly triumphant; and for humbler claim
> Of that imaginative impulse sent
> From these majestic floods, yon shining cliffs,
> The untransmuted shapes of many worlds,
> Cerulean ether's pure inhabitants,
> These forests unapproachable by death,
> That shall endure as long as man endures,
> To think, to hope, to worship, and to feel,

> To struggle, to be lost within himself
> In trepidation, from the blank abyss
> To look with bodily eyes, and be consoled.'

> (6:456–71)

The stones of the convent and the cross of Jesus standing erect "as if / Hands of angelic powers had fixed it there" take their place with mountains, stars, and forests as things upon which man can look with bodily eyes and take comfort in the permanence they seem to symbolize. Nature's images, and those made with hands, stimulate the same kind of "imaginative impulse"—hence, perhaps, nature's intervention. But the consolation Wordsworth indicates is not securely grounded, for we know that there is corruption in the stars and spruce budworm in the forests, and the convent of Chartreuse is "from the undiscriminating sweep / And rage of one state whirlwind, insecure." Wordsworth returns to the topic later in *The Prelude,* 9:465–75.

> And sometimes—
> When to a convent in a meadow green,
> By a brook-side, we came, a roofless pile,
> And not by reverential touch of Time
> Dismantled, but by violence abrupt—
> In spite of those heart-bracing colloquies,
> In spite of real fervour, and of that
> Less genuine and wrought up within myself—
> I could not but bewail a wrong so harsh,
> And for the Matin-bell to sound no more
> Grieved.

As symbols of permanence, unless one is already a believing Christian, the church, the cross, and the bell will not do. Cromwell, Robespierre, and the Ministry of Cults will make short work of them.

It is really quite astonishing that the city of London, which seems so entirely concerned with temporal and material affairs, should do better as a symbol of permanence than

the convent of Chartreuse. Yet this is what Wordsworth
seems to imply in *The Prelude,* 8:543–59.

> On the roof
> Of an itinerant vehicle I sate,
> With vulgar men about me, trivial forms
> Of houses, pavements, streets, of men and things,—
> Mean shapes on every side: but, at the instant,
> When to myself it fairly might be said,
> The threshold now is overpast, (how strange
> That ought external to the living mind
> Should have such mighty sway! yet so it was),
> A weight of ages did at once descend
> Upon my heart; no thought embodied, no
> Distinct remembrances, but weight and power,—
> Power growing under weight: alas! I feel
> That I am trifling: 'twas a moment's pause,—
> All that took place within me came and went
> As in a moment; yet with Time it dwells,
> And grateful memòry, as a thing divine.

Wordsworth leaves the reader much to question in these
lines. What was his experience on this occasion, and what
comment on, or explanation of, the experience is he offering
in these lines? The sonnet "Composed upon Westminster
Bridge," which seems to have the same origin, is no help in
answering these questions, for it develops quite differently.
All one can safely deduce is that the emotion felt seems to
have no sufficient cause. "Vulgar men . . . and things," "trivial forms," "mean shapes"—these sights should produce
mean and vulgar effects or the effects of disgust and withdrawal, yet Wordsworth felt "weight and power, / Power
growing under weight." And this thing of weight and power
seems to be something that Wordsworth thinks we should
expect to recognize only within the human mind itself. In
fact, he distrusts (or pretends to distrust) the experience: "I
feel / That I am trifling." Nevertheless, he says of the moment: "with Time it dwells." We must not slip over this

statement. It probably does not mean simply that the experience was unforgettable, for the next phrase ("And grateful memory") seems to be something more than a mere apposition. And what does he mean by adding "as a thing divine?" A thing divine, according to traditional ways of thinking, should dwell in the permanence of God, secure from time. Is the phrase "with Time it dwells" meant to signify that whatever was gained in the moment cannot be lost? Does it belong, in T. S. Eliot's phrase in "Burnt Norton," "where past and future are gathered"? Wordsworth's expressions are imprecise enough to allow us to fill in meanings like this if we want to.

Some people would be inclined to dismiss the matter as an attempt to impose a sense of importance on the experience by means of an insistent vagueness, much as Joseph Conrad does in certain passages of *Heart of Darkness,* when he speaks of "monstrous passions," "unspeakable rites," and so on. But Wordsworth's vagueness differs from Conrad's in important respects. Although "weight" and "power" are presented as unattached qualities—we can neither put a name to nor with any certainty say we acknowledge the feeling that is weighty and powerful—they nevertheless have a certain precision when we consider them as antitheses to the earlier epithets ("mean," "vulgar," and "trivial") which had quite specific attachments. And though Wordsworth cannot particularize the feeling, he is careful to bring out the paradoxical nature of its occasion. That the streets of a brash and dirty city should call forth that particular experience, and that such an experience should be felt in so brief a moment—how paradoxical! There is in such a paradox a strong and obvious implication that what is experienced is noble and immutable.

Nevertheless, if we want to particularize any further, we must retreat to guesswork. A clue, possibly, is in the business of the threshold. Once he has crossed Westminster Bridge, and is, as he seems to say, really in London, things no longer seem to Wordsworth vulgar or trivial. "A weight of ages did at once descend / Upon my heart." This weight is probably, as I suggested in chapter 6, a sudden access of historical consciousness. Men organize themselves, rule kingdoms, and build towers, domes, and temples with their eyes on a time scale vastly bigger than their individual lives, and it hardly ever occurs to anyone that it is rather odd that they should do so. It is understandable that men should wish to secure the lifetime of the children and grandchildren whom they know, but they build and plan beyond the lifetime of their great-grandchildren, and there is really no satisfactory explanation of why they do. Yet, while the fact argues nothing about human immortality, it does point out that men have another time scale in their consciousness than the one that is immediately and personally relevant to them. To that extent, the sight of London may have suggested something to Wordsworth concerning permanence.

When we review the images we have so far dealt with, we may well think that none of them is really satisfactory. The seasons can be seen as a pulse, or cycles of time. But cycles are countable, and even if their pattern of renewal suggests an inexhaustible energy, they are, simply because we count them, measures of our own decay. Waterfalls and glaciers suggest natural processes as strongly as they suggest permanence; if we look at them carefully we can see where they have changed course, cut new channels in the rocks, and left their stalactites and moraines. Churches are symbols of eternity only to believers, and great cities have submitted to the sand or the jungle. All these things belong to the world of sense and phenomena and are subject to its weathering. Only imperfectly, then, can they suggest independence of such a world. To do more than this, phenomena must to some extent deceive the observer; only by way of metaphor can time suggest the timeless.

Given these conditions, can the world of objects afford any kind of vision or experience which not merely suggests the notion of a timeless vantage point, but disturbs the emotions and imagination in a manner which suggests an actual experience of timelessness? I must call on William James yet again. In his third Gifford lecture on religious experience, he quotes an unnamed contributor to a collection of depositions concerning mystical experience.

> I have on a number of occasions felt that I enjoyed a period of intimate communion with the divine. These meetings came unasked and unexpected, and seemed to consist merely in the temporary obliteration of the conventionalities which usually surround and cover my life. . . . Once it was when from the summit of a high mountain I looked over a gashed and corrugated landscape extending to a long convex of ocean that ascended to the horizon, and again from the same point when I could see nothing beneath me but a boundless expanse of white cloud, on the blown surface of which a few high peaks, including the one I was on, seemed plunging about as if they were dragging their anchors. What I felt on these occasions was a temporary loss of my own identity, accompanied by an illumination which revealed to me deeper significance than I had been wont to attach to life. It is in this that I find my justification for saying that I have enjoyed communication with God. Of course, the absence of such a being as this would be chaos. I cannot conceive of life without its presence.[1]

Without doubting the honesty of the contributor, I am bound to wonder whether both the experience and the interpretation might have been molded by *The Prelude,* 14:38–56, which it so markedly resembles. Wordsworth and two companions were climbing Snowdon by night, in order to see the sunrise. It was a warm, misty night, and visibility was poor, but suddenly the ground at the climbers' feet brightened as they emerged above the layer of cloud, and

> instantly a light upon the turf
> Fell like a flash, and lo! as I looked up,
> The Moon hung naked in a firmament
> Of azure without cloud, and at my feet
> Rested a silent sea of hoary mist.
> A hundred hills their dusky backs upheaved

All over this still ocean; and beyond,
Far, far beyond, the solid vapours stretched,
In headlands, tongues, and promontory shapes,
Into the main Atlantic, that appeared
To dwindle, and give up his majesty,
Usurped upon far as the sight could reach.
Not so the ethereal vault; encroachment none
Was there, nor loss; only the inferior stars
Had disappeared, or shed a fainter light
In the clear presence of the full-orbed Moon,
Who, from her sovereign elevation, gazed
Upon the billowy ocean, as it lay
All meek and silent...

In both accounts, a mountainous landscape near the sea, viewed from a peak above the clouds, is seen to be remarkably like the sea itself, studded with ships or islands. Neither author actually mistakes the landscape for the sea, but each is impressed by the similarity. This perception leads the observer to an intensified conviction of the existence of God. (Wordsworth speaks of the vision in lines 66–67 as "the type / Of a majestic intellect.") Neither author represents his exalted moment as a conversion experience. For both of them it seems to be a matter of added conviction, of a deeper understanding of the nature of a God in whom they are already disposed to believe.

If we are to understand why such a result follows such an experience, we must examine very carefully the feeling implicit in both accounts. Neither author mentions pleasure, yet I am certain that both felt so great a joy in the vision that the words "joy" and "pleasure" were useless to them. And the pleasure is certainly aesthetic. The prose climbs to the threshold of poetry: "a gashed and corrugated landscape"; "expanse of white cloud, on the blown surface of which a few high peaks... seemed plunging about as if they were dragging their anchors." In Wordsworth's account the similes are compressed into metaphors; the expanse of white cloud is a "silent sea of hoary mist," and the high peaks are "headlands, tongues, and promontory shapes." Both authors seem obtrusively to assert the images they use, because for both of them the special character of the scene does not lie in the beauty which it has in itself, but in its dramatic general resemblance to something else.

Again I must stress that neither author is actually mistaken about what he sees. Both accounts plainly indicate that the resemblance is never close enough really to deceive the senses. An expanse of white cloud in fact looks nothing like the sea. A "billowy ocean" cannot be "meek and silent." And above all, the real thing is there, distant but visible, and still obviously different from the things that simulate it: "a gashed and corrugated landscape extending to a long convex of ocean"; "the solid vapours stretched . . . Into the main Atlantic, that appeared / To dwindle and give up his majesty." It is in fact the character of the scenes as visual metaphors that excites both authors, and it is from this that the religious value of the experiences seems to derive.

The first author describes his reaction only in general terms; he has clearly not tried to impose a detailed meaning on what he is remembering. But he does make one uncompromising assertion: "I have enjoyed communication with God . . . the absence of such a being as this would be chaos." The peculiar feature of this conviction is that the author has just had an experience that might suggest that the sense data the universe presents to him is not always reliable. It is not simply a matter of the white cloud looking something like the sea; there is also a partial disturbance of the sense of equilibrium. If we are in a stationary train and the train on the next line begins to pull out of the station, we may, if we happen not to turn our eyes to the platform on the other side, be deluded into believing that our train is moving. James's author seems to have experienced a similar delusion—the movement of the cloud masses is so large-scale that it seems that the protruding peaks are moving. "A few high peaks, including the one I was one, seemed plunging about as if they were dragging their anchors."

This was a delightful misconception, no doubt, but one would expect it to be also a little alarming. The illusion that the ground beneath his feet was plunging about must have brought with it a kind of drunken vertigo and some physical fear. But James's author seems entirely transported by his illusion. It adds to his sense that the universe is rational and ordered because it was made by God, yet all he has been saying points to the idea that the world presented to us by the senses is more chaotic than we normally think. His conclusion seems perverse. But of course the thing to remember is that his illusion has the nature of an artistic deception. The commonplace example of the moving train disturbs us because we are completely, if momentarily, deluded. But when we are aware that a representation is a representation, we are in varying degrees delighted with it.

It is something of a mystery why we take pleasure in being partially and willingly deceived and why we take pleasure in figurative language. It is, perhaps, a sense of enrichment in being aware of several worlds at once. Insofar as the illusion is practiced on us by other men and women, we are delighted, among other reasons, because something is revealed of human capability by their skill in deceiving, and our cooperation in being deceived and yet remaining in our senses. This kind of known deception is also an agreed deception, a necessary protocol between us and the artist. What, however, are we to make of the known but apparently random deceptions experienced by Wordsworth and James's author? We may, indeed, make nothing of them; we may think of them as entirely accidental, the fortuitous universe throwing up fortuitous occasions of delight in the course of its aimless changes. But the two authors think otherwise. God is the implicit, hidden artist with whom, in the act of perceiving and understanding, they have cooperated. And it is God as an artist who is inferred here, not the First Cause. What each author has seen is a visual metaphor. The likeness is agreed, while the greater difference remains known. God has invited cooperation in the manner of an artist; human sense must, in Wordsworth's phrase, "half-perceive and half-create" such a spectacle as this. It is this sharing in the act of creation, perhaps, which James's author senses as communication with God.

The conviction of a divine artistic power recognized in this experience also resolves the paradox of the prose author seeing the universe as being controlled by God at the very moment when that universe appears to be deceptive and untrustworthy. The artist's greatness lies in his control of form; God, being a perfect artist, has perfect control of an infinitude of forms; he is eternally shaping and reshaping his medium. "The absence of such a being as this would be chaos."

I have paid so much attention to James's author in order to show that the kind of experience he describes, and the kind of conclusions he draws from it, are, though by no means commonplace, not peculiar to Wordsworth. I must now examine two important differences between the poetic and the prose accounts. James's author seems on both occasions to have climbed in daylight; Wordsworth climbed at night, beginning in a misty darkness. The prose author claims the experience as a communication with God; Wordsworth does not name God, but he does go into some detail about the nature of the unnamed being. Wordsworth's ascent in darkness must have been hazardous, even with a local guide, and required a certain amount of courage. His account is entirely matter-of-fact, but it is possible to see the dark journey as a kind of adventure of faith and the sudden moonlight as an unlooked-for reward for perseverance. But the real point of the moonlight is the great difference it makes to the appearance of things, not only in contrast to the misty darkness of a few moments before, but also in contrast to a normal daylight view—both of the specific landscape he describes and of a seascape such as moon and cloud now conspire to suggest to the responsive imagination. In other words, the point of the description is simply to emphasize how different the scene is from the reality which it nevertheless so strongly suggests. The paradox inherent in metaphor—"the observa-

tion of affinities / In objects where no brotherhood exists"—
is for Wordsworth the very stuff of literature. He makes plain
the element of paradox in the phrase "solid vapours," but he
also goes further. For a moment the illusion is greater than
the reality.

> the solid vapours stretched,
> In headlands, tongues, and promontory shapes,
> Into the main Atlantic, that appeared
> To dwindle, and give up his majesty,
> Usurped upon far as the sight could reach.

The significance of the supreme importance that the poetry
attributes to the illusion reveals itself in the differences between Wordsworth's and the prose author's conclusions about
their experiences. For the latter, the hidden artist is quite
simply God; for Wordsworth, he is "the type / Of a majestic
intellect." At this point we need to read a little more of
Wordsworth's comment on his experience, for it revealed not
merely that God's mind is like a human mind, but that it is
particularly like one in its greatest power, its endless artistic
creativity.

> There I beheld the emblem of a mind
> That feeds upon infinity, that broods
> Over the dark abyss, intent to hear
> Its voices issuing forth to silent light
> In one continuous stream; a mind sustained
> By recognitions of transcendent power,
> In sense conducting to ideal form,
> In soul of more than mortal privilege.
> One function, above all, of such a mind
> Had Nature shadowed there, by putting forth,
> 'Mid circumstances awful and sublime,
> That mutual domination which she loves
> To exert upon the face of outward things,
> So moulded, joined, abstracted, so endowed
> With interchangeable supremacy,

That men, least sensitive, see, hear, perceive,
And cannot choose but feel.

(14:70–86)

The "majestic intellect," the "mind / That feeds upon infinity," is a human mind, and in particular the mind of artistic genius. What nature "shadows" in such a splendid vision is a mind like that of a human artist, an intellect like that of the most majestic human intellect. But what is the "it" that appears to be the type of such an intellect? The immediate answer—"the whole spectacle"—may well be the right one, for this seems to be what Wordsworth is trying to say. But another answer is possible. What, we might ask in a medieval sort of way, is the proximate cause of the vision? The answer is the moon. Moonlight reveals the forms and casts the shadows on which the human imagination can work. And the suddenness with which the moon breaks through gives the Snowdon path a moment's affinity with the Damascus road.

> instantly a light upon the turf
> Fell like a flash, and lo! as I looked up,
> The Moon hung naked in a firmament...

These lines seem to carry with them a shock of sudden awe and an immediate Pauline rapture. But in case we suspect that we have been giving these lines too great an importance, let us look a little further on in the passage. Those "solid vapours," stretching among the "promontory shapes" to the sea itself, diminish the Atlantic, but

> Not so the ethereal vault; encroachment none
> Was there, nor loss; only the inferior stars
> Had disappeared, or shed a fainter light
> In the clear presence of the full-orbed Moon,
> Who, from her sovereign elevation, gazed
> Upon the billowy ocean.

Everything in these lines, but particularly the words "presence," "full-orbed," and "sovereign elevation," suggests that the moon is the monarch of heaven; she gazes on the sea of cloud beneath as God looked on his handiwork at the creation; she gives it form, light, shadow, and reflection. She and the heaven wherein she dwells are untouched by the changes over which she presides. And beneath the sea of cloud is "A fixed, abysmal, gloomy breathing-place" (l. 58). The moon broods over this dark abyss as God's majestic intellect broods over the universe he has created: the moon's "sovereign elevation" is the timeless vantage point from which God views time. But the moon is also the type of man's intellect and her elevation is also the timeless vantage point from which man as an artist views the perpetually new creation which his mind and God's "with blended might / Accomplish." Wordsworth, in this passage, sees God's mind as unceasingly creative and formative; world without end he fashions perfect shapes and images "in sense conducting to ideal form." The universe is both his creation and his medium; he exerts his artistic domination "on the face of outward things." The forms are always changing yet are always perfect; God's is an "interchangeable supremacy." He himself is unchanged in his "sovereign elevation." The timeless moments man experiences are moments of sharing in the first act of creation. Wordsworth sees this artistic partnership between man and God much as it is perceived in Proverbs 8:29–31.

> When he laid down the foundations of the earth
> I was by his side, a master craftsman,
> delighting him day after day,
> ever at play in his presence,
> at play everywhere in his world.

It is perhaps now possible to make a cautious surmise about the nature of the timeless moment as Wordsworth experienced it. It consists in a brief and elusive but nevertheless total change in the manner of seeing reality: the universe of space and time, that "remorseless" thing, is no longer seen as a cloud of fortuitous systems or a device constructed and set going by some remote and loveless engineer, but as a sort of infinite metaphor, the poetry of God. One need not share the beliefs which make this vision possible in order to see the potency of the shift in consciousness, its capacity for consequential fruits. We do not need to agree that it is an escape from prison; it is an escape from the feel of prison. And there seems little harm in that.

Appendix:
The Ruined Shrines

There is good reason to suppose that Wordsworth as a boy had some knowledge of the history of the shrines he visited. Such ruins become part of the folklore of the district in which they are situated, and the kind of boy who thinks it worthwhile to spend a day's holiday visiting them is the sort who will absorb such folklore. There is also reason to suppose a more formal and detailed knowledge. Hawkshead Grammar School, which Wordsworth attended from 1779 to 1787, was firmly religious in its origin and tradition. Its headmasters were graduates of Cambridge and clergymen in the Church of England. Moreover, the school's founder, Edwin Sandys, had suffered exile for his Protestant faith during the reign of Mary Tudor, subsequently becoming archbishop of York under Elizabeth. It would be strange if the pupils of Hawkshead did not have some grounding in Reformation history, and some particular knowledge of how the religious upheaval had affected the northwest of England.

I argued in chapter 6 that two features of Wordsworth's experiences at these shrines were a sudden onset of historical consciousness and a sense of a mystical persistence of the tradition of prayer among the ruins. I hope that the reader may get a better sense of these features with the help of the following brief historical sketches.

CARTMEL PRIORY (1805 version of *The Prelude,* 10: 493)

Although Wordsworth does not describe any experience as being specifically connected with Cartmel Priory, we know that he once visited the grave of his old schoolmaster in the priory churchyard. It is likely too that he had visited Cartmel earlier with his schoolboy companions, since it is en route to other shrines which he mentions. There is something in the history of the priory, and its condition at the time of his visits, that may have contributed to that sense of spiritual persistence in the midst of decay that he evokes in connection with other ruins. It was founded by William Marshall the elder, baron of Cartmel, and later earl of Pembroke, in 1188 for the Canons Regular of Saint Augustine. We know little of its history, but what we do know is interesting. Marshall stipulated in his original foundation that an altar should be provided, with a priest "for the people." When in 1537 Henry VIII's commissioners turned out the brethren, and, with the same good business sense as modern thieves, stripped the lead off the church roof, Marshall's apparently minor condition faced them with a problem which they had to refer to London.

The provision of an altar and priest for the people constituted a parochial right. The authorities in London reminded their Cartmel agents that Henry's law was passed to dissolve monasteries, not parish churches, and in the case of Cartmel parochial right was proved. However, instead of the nave being allowed, as was usual in such cases, the south aisle of the choir, known as the Town Choir, continued to serve as the parish church. Thus religious services were regularly performed in a section of an otherwise ruined church.

In 1618, a George Preston began the work of restoration. The church was reroofed and presented with an oak screen and canopies which were placed on top of the choir stalls and misericords which had survived eighty years of ruin.[1] However in the next two hundred years nothing was done, and the church fell into ruin again. The Lancashire historian Dunham Whitaker, visiting it in the early nineteenth century, felt that the time was ripe for another Preston.[2] Presumably the Town Choir was still being used for services at the time of Wordsworth's visits, and it is not unreasonable to suppose that he knew this. It is also not unreasonable to suppose that he may have perceived a certain symbol in the tumbled stones and debris of a church which, through centuries of decay, maintained its consecrated status and function. Such a symbol may have been a part of the mystical experiences associated with other ruins, or may at least have shaped his memory of them at the time of writing.

LADY HOLME (*The Prelude*, 2:54–65)

Lady Holme island is situated on Lake Windermere, a few hundred yards off the Bowness shore, and its shrine was a chauntry. The first mention of it in historical documents occurs in an *inquisition post mortem* into the property of Walter de Lyndesay in 1272. He held, among other things, the lake known as Wynandermer, containing an island with a *mansio* (Holme Island, now called Belle Isle), together with fishing rights in the River Kent. Out of the income accruing, a stipend of ten marks a year in perpetuity was to be paid to the hermit brethren of Lady Holme by the charter of the said Walter. Since there was no mention of a house or a chauntry in the previous will, that of William de Lancastre, we can date the shrine between 1246 and 1272. According to de Lyndesay's charter, mass was to be celebrated every day for the souls of his parents, his uncle William de Lancastre, for all the faithful departed, and for the well-being of himself and his family in this life and the next.³

The chauntry was probably served by two priests, who no doubt eked out their yearly ten marks by tilling the land on the Bowness shore. In the third quarter of the fourteenth century, following the Black Death that killed half the parish priests in northern England, the chauntry was vacant. It was probably abolished shortly after the dissolution of the monasteries, and by the time Wordsworth visited the island all that remained, according to the 1805 *Prelude,* was "An old stone table, and a moulder'd Cave" (l. 64). But the island's tradition of prayer and meditation was revived briefly in the early 1780s, when William Wilberforce, the leader of the forces in the British House of Commons who were pressing for the abolition of the slave trade, then living at Rayrigg, used to row every morning to the island to think and pray. During the same period, Wordsworth and his friends used to row to the island in their schoolboy races. If Wordsworth had encountered the great emancipator on one of these occasions he would certainly have told us; nevertheless, the coincidence itself is, for the reader, a curious adjunct to Wordsworth's ambiguous hint that the island was still "served / Daily with chaunted rites."

FURNESS ABBEY (*The Prelude,* 2:94–137)

Founded in 1123 by Stephen, count of Boulogne and Mortain, later King Stephen of England, Furness Abbey was originally sited at Tulketh, near Preston, for monks of the Order of Savigny, and was moved to Furness in 1127. Twenty years later the Order of Savigny amalgamated with the Cistercian order. The abbey's possessions included most of the peninsula of Furness (though not Cartmel), with forests to the north and rich agricultural land to the south. Wordsworth makes much of the secluded position of the abbey, praising "the deep shelter that is there, and such / The safeguard for repose and quietness." He would surely know enough about the history of the abbey to know how well this seclusion had served the brethren. Sited as it was between Morecambe Bay and the hills of Cumberland, the abbey was so isolated that one medieval clerk recorded it as being on an island. Furness had originally been granted many feudal privileges and in the course of time augmented these, so that it became very independent. This autonomy was greatly strengthened by freedom from interference, since royal officials had to cross the Way of the Sands—a deterrent to frequent officious visitation.

The abbey was, however, more vulnerable to attacks from the north. The abbot built Peel Castle as a defense against the Scots, who for a long time disputed the border. In spite of this, the abbey prospered and grew munificent. In the last years before the Dissolution, the abbey's tenants would bring twenty or thirty horses to take away sixty weekly barrels of beer, and with each barrel a dozen loaves. Thirty or forty carts would take away manure for the tenants' fields in Newbarn and Hawcoat. Every tenant with a plough had the privilege of sending two people to dine in the abbey once a week between Martinmas and Whitsuntide. For the children of tenants, the abbey provided a grammar school and also taught singing. Thirteen poor men were kept as almsmen.

Eventually, in 1537, the brethren of Furness surrendered their abbey to Henry VIII's minister, Thomas Cromwell, to whom some of its lands were granted.[4]

Notes

Chapter One

1. David Perkins, *The Quest for Permanence.*
2. Dorothy Wordsworth, *The Journals of Dorothy Wordsworth,* ed. Helen Darbishire, pp. 201–2.
3. David Perkins, *Wordsworth and the Poetry of Sincerity,* p. 24.
4. Virginia Woolf, *Orlando;* quoted by C. A. Patrides in *Aspects of Time* (Manchester: Manchester University Press, 1976), p. 1.
5. Herbert Lindenberger, *On Wordsworth's "Prelude,"* pp. 199, 201–4.
6. Ibid., p. 169.
7. Melvin Rader, *Wordsworth,* pp. 6–9, 16–21.
8. Ibid., pp. 21, 22.
9. Coleridge, *Anima Poetae,* quoted by Rader in *Wordsworth,* p. 23.
10. E. L. Stelzig, *All Shades of Consciousness,* p. 119.
11. William Wordsworth, *The Prelude,* ed. Ernest de Selincourt, rev. Helen Darbishire (Oxford: Oxford University Press, 1959), p. lvii.
12. Paul D. Sheats, *The Making of Wordsworth's Poetry, 1785–1798,* pp. 173–80.
13. Jonathan Wordsworth, *The Music of Humanity,* p. 23.
14. Ibid., pp. 27–28.

Chapter Two

1. Lindenberger, *On Wordsworth's "Prelude,"* p. 137.
2. Geoffrey Durrant, *Wordsworth and the Great System*, p. 63.
3. Bernard Blackstone, *The Lost Travellers*, pp. 10, 20.
4. Ibid., p. 9.
5. S. T. Coleridge, *Biographia Literaria*, ed. Ernest Rhys (London and Toronto: Dent, 1927), p. 161.
6. Perkins, *Wordsworth and the Poetry of Sincerity*, p. 25.
7. Durrant, *Wordsworth and the Great System*, p. 145.

Chapter Three

1. Robert Browning, "Bishop Blougram's Apology"; see ll. 210–16.
2. Alan Grob, *The Philosophic Mind*, p. 47.
3. Ibid., pp. 59–60.
4. Durrant, *Wordsworth and the Great System*, pp. 90–91.
5. Perkins, *Wordsworth and the Poetry of Sincerity*, p. 129.
6. R. J. Onorato, *The Character of the Poet: Wordsworth in "The Prelude"* (Princeton, N.J.: Princeton University Press, 1971), pp. 34, 64.
7. Perkins, *Wordsworth and the Poetry of Sincerity*, p. 3; E. D. Hirsch, *Wordsworth and Schelling*, p. 15.
8. Grob, *Philosophic Mind*, p. 49.
9. Newton P. Stallknecht, *Strange Seas of Thought*, p. 223.
10. Durrant, *Wordsworth and the Great System*, pp. 152–53.
11. Stallknecht, *Strange Seas of Thought*, pp. 24, 65.
12. Ibid., p. 126.
13. Geoffrey Hartman, *Wordsworth's Poetry, 1787–1814*, pp. 39, 41, 48.
14. Sir Matthew Hale, *Primitive Origination of Mankind*, quoted by Stallknecht in *Strange Seas of Thought*, p. 49.
15. Arthur Beatty, *William Wordsworth*.
16. John F. Danby, *William Wordsworth*, pp. 16–17.
17. Thomas De Quincey, *Selected Writings of Thomas De Quincey*, ed. Philip Van Doren Stern (New York: Random House, 1949), p. 422.
18. Not everyone agrees. Danby, for instance, says: "The mad dervish . . . is not an isolate. His aim is to rescue and preserve the record of man's total work. His immediate fellows, their wives and children he is willing to sacrifice. Nevertheless he acts from a sense of responsibility. He is answerable to the larger community in time. He carries with him the inheritance of man's best achievement: the time-

transcending truth man has responded to" (*William Wordsworth,* p. 14).

19. Hans Meyerhoff, *Time in Literature;* see especially chapter 2, "Direction and Death," pp. 64–84.

Chapter Four

1. Hartman, *Wordsworth's Poetry,* p. 38.
2. William Wordsworth, *Poems,* ed. Philip Wayne, 3 vols. (London: Dent, 1955), 1:xvi.
3. Blackstone, *Lost Travellers,* p. 93.
4. Sheats, *Making of Wordsworth's Poetry,* p. 147.
5. Ibid., p. 142.
6. John Garetson Dings, *The Mind in Its Place,* p. 126.
7. Danby, *William Wordsworth,* p. 29.

Chapter Five

1. To William Matthews, Sept. 23, 1791, and Nov. 23, 1791; Ernest de Selincourt, ed., *Letters of William and Dorothy Wordsworth,* 2d rev. ed., vol. 1, *The Early Years,* pp. 59, 62.
2. F. R. Leavis, "Revaluations (VI): Wordsworth," *Scrutiny* 3 (1963): 234–57.
3. William James, *The Varieties of Religious Experience,* pp. 23, 29.
4. William Empson, *Seven Types of Ambiguity,* pp. 49–51.

Chapter Six

1. Perkins, *Wordsworth and the Poetry of Sincerity,* p. 5.
2. William F. Lynch, *Christ and Apollo,* p. 44.
3. Rene Descartes, *Philosophical Writings: A Selection,* trans. and ed. by E. Anscombe and P. T. Geach, with an Introduction by A. Koyre (Edinburgh: Nelson, 1954), p. 88.
4. For a more professional exposition of this point, see L. J. Beck, *The Metaphysics of Descartes,* pp. 192–98.
5. Blackstone, *Lost Travellers,* p. 93.
6. Ibid.; and William Hale White, *An Examination of the Charge of Apostasy against Wordsworth,* p. 61.
7. Lindenberger, *On Wordsworth's "Prelude,"* p. 153.

8. Katherine Chorley, "Cumberland (including Furness)," in *The English Counties,* new ed., rev. B. Webster Smith (London: Odhams, 1963).

9. Canon S. Taylor, *Cartmel: People and Priory* (Kendal: privately published, 1955).

10. Ernest de Selincourt and Helen Darbishire, eds., *The Prelude,* p. 398.

11. Ibid., p. 198n.

12. James, *Varieties of Religious Experience,* p. 228.

13. Ibid., p. 53.

14. Ibid., p. 293.

Chapter Seven

1. James, *Varieties of Religious Experience,* p. 70.

Appendix

1. L. G. F. Dykes and T. Hardwick, *The Priory Church of St Michael and St Mary* (Cartmel: privately published, 1955).

2. Thomas Dunham Whitaker, *An Account of the Parish of Cartmel* (London: Nichols, Son, and Bentley, 1818).

3. A. P. Brydson, *Sidelights on Mediaeval Windermere* (Kendal: privately published, 1911).

4. Charles M. Jopling, *Sketch Of Furness and Cartmel* (Ulverston, privately published, 1843); J. C. Dickinson, *Furness Abbey* (London and Gloucester: British Publishing Co., 1965); Chorley, "Cumberland (including Furness)," in *English Counties.*

Selected Bibliography

The following is a list of books and articles which I have found either genuinely helpful or in some way stimulating.

Beatty, Arthur. *William Wordsworth: His Doctrine and Art in Their Historical Relations.* Madison, Wis.: University of Wisconsin Press, 1960.

Beck, L. J. *The Metaphysics of Descartes.* Oxford: Oxford University Press, 1965.

Blackstone, Bernard. *The Lost Travellers.* London: Longmans, 1962.

Bloom, Harold. *The Visionary Company.* Garden City, N.Y.: Cornell University Press, 1963.

Bostetter, E. E. *The Romantic Ventriloquists: Wordsworth, Coleridge, Keats, Shelley, Byron.* Seattle, Wash.: University of Washington Press, 1963.

Clarke, C. C. *The Romantic Paradox.* London: Routledge and Kegan Paul, 1960.

Danby, John F. *William Wordsworth: "The Prelude" and Other Poems.* London: Edward Arnold, 1963.

———. *The Simple Wordsworth.* London: Routledge and Kegan Paul, 1960.

de Selincourt, Ernest, ed. *Letters of William and Dorothy Wordsworth.* 6 vols. Oxford: Oxford University Press, 1935–39. 2d ed. rev. by C. L. Shaver et al., 1967–.

Dings, John Garetson. *The Mind in Its Place: Wordsworth's "Michael" and the Poetry of 1800.* Salzburg: Humanities Press, 1973.

Durrant, Geoffrey. *Wordsworth and the Great System.* Cambridge: Cambridge University Press, 1970.

Empson, William. *Seven Types of Ambiguity.* London: Chatto and Windus, 1956.

Ferry, David. *The Limits of Mortality.* Middletown, Conn.: Wesleyan University Press, 1959.

Garber, Frederick. *Wordsworth and the Poetry of Encounter.* Urbana, Ill.: University of Illinois Press, 1971.

Grob, Alan. *The Philosophic Mind: A Study of Wordsworth's Poetry and Thought, 1797–1805.* Columbus, Ohio: Ohio State University Press, 1973.

――――. "Wordsworth and Godwin: A Reassessment." *Studies in Romanticism* 6 (1967):98–119.

Hartman, Geoffrey. *Wordsworth's Poetry 1787–1814.* New Haven, Conn.: Yale University Press, 1964.

Havens, R. D. *The Mind of a Poet: A Study of Wordsworth's Thought with Reference to "The Prelude."* Baltimore, Md.: Johns Hopkins, 1941.

Hirsch, E. D. *Wordsworth and Schelling.* New Haven, Conn.: Yale University Press, 1960.

James, D. G. *Scepticism and Poetry.* London: Allen and Unwin, 1937.

James, William. *The Varieties of Religious Experience.* New York: New American Library, Mentor, 1958.

Jones, John. *The Egotistical Sublime: A History of Wordsworth's Imagination.* London: Chatto and Windus, 1954.

Lindenberger, Herbert. *On Wordsworth's "Prelude."* Princeton, N.J.: Princeton University Press, 1963.

Lynch, William F. *Christ and Apollo.* South Bend, Ind.: Notre Dame University Press, 1975.

Meyerhoff, Hans. *Time in Literature.* Berkeley, Cal.: University of California Press, 1955.

Moorman, Mary. *William Wordsworth: A Biography.* 2 vols. Vol. 1. *The Early Years, 1770–1803.* Oxford: Oxford University Press, 1957. Vol. 2. *The Later Years, 1803–1850.* Oxford: Oxford University Press, 1965.

Perkins, David. *The Quest for Permanence.* Cambridge, Mass.: Harvard University Press, 1969.

――――. *Wordsworth and the Poetry of Sincerity.* Cambridge, Mass.: Harvard University Press, 1964.

Piper, H. W. *The Active Universe: Pantheism and the Concept of the Imagination in the English Romantic Poets.* London: University of London, Athlone Press, 1962.

Poulet, Georges. *Studies in Human Time.* Translated by Elliot Coleman. Baltimore, Md.: Johns Hopkins, 1956.

Rader, Melvin. *Wordsworth: A Philosophical Approach.* Oxford: Oxford University Press, 1967.

Raysor, Thomas. "The Themes of Immortality." *PMLA* 69 (1954):861–75.

Salvesen, Christopher. *The Landscape of Memory.* Lincoln, Neb.: University of Nebraska Press, 1965.

Schneider, B. R. *Wordsworth's Cambridge Education.* Cambridge: Cambridge University Press, 1957.

Sheats, Paul D. *The Making of Wordsworth's Poetry, 1785–1798.* Cambridge, Mass.: Harvard University Press, 1973.

Stallknecht, Newton P. *Strange Seas of Thought: Studies in Wordsworth's Philosophy of Man and Nature.* Bloomington, Ind.: Indiana University Press, 1958.

Stelzig, E. L. *All Shades of Consciousness: Wordsworth's Poetry and the Self in Time.* The Hague: Humanities Press, 1975.

Trilling, Lionel. "Wordsworth and the Iron Time." In *Wordsworth: Centenary Studies,* ed. Gilbert T. Dunklin (Princeton, N.J.: Princeton University Press, 1951), pp. 131–52.

Tuveson, E. L. *The Imagination as a Means of Grace.* Berkeley, Cal.: University of California Press, 1960.

White, William Hale. *An Examination of the Charge of Apostasy against Wordsworth.* London, 1898. Reprint. Folcroft, Pa.: Folcroft Library Editions, 1973.

Wordsworth, Dorothy. *The Journals of Dorothy Wordsworth.* Edited by Helen Darbishire. Oxford: Oxford University Press, 1958.

Wordsworth, Jonathan. *The Music of Humanity: A Critical Study of Wordsworth's "Ruined Cottage."* London: Nelson, 1969.

Index

Wordsworth's poems are listed here by title or first line in the form used in the de Selincourt-Darbishire edition.

English by birth, Jeffrey Baker was educated at Manchester University, from which he has received a B.A. with honors (1947), M.A. (1965), and Ph.D. (1970). Formerly senior lecturer in English at Manchester Polytechnic, he is currently associate professor of English at St. Francis Xavier University in Nova Scotia. His earlier studies of Wordsworth's poetry include articles in *Criticism* and the *Antigonish Review*.

The manuscript was edited by Sherwyn T. Carr. The book was designed by Don Ross. The typeface for the text is Bembo, based on a cut by Francesco Griffo for the Venetian printer Aldus Manutius about 1495. The display face is Garamond, designed by Claude Garamond about 1532.

The text is printed on 60 lb. Booktext Natural text paper, and the book is bound in Holliston Mills' Kingston Natural Finish cloth over binder's boards. Manufactured in the United States of America.